EYEWITNESS *TRAVEL GUIDES*

THAI
PHRASE BOOK

D
LONDON • NE... SYDNEY • MOSCOW

A DORLING KINDERSLEY BOOK

Compiled by Lexus Ltd with David and Somsong Smyth

Set in 9/9 Plantin and Plantin Light by Lexus Ltd
with Typesetters Ltd, Hertford
Printed in Great Britain by Cambus Litho

First published in Great Britain in 1997
by Dorling Kindersley Limited
9 Henrietta Street, London WC2E 8PS

A CIP catalogue record is available from the British Library.
ISBN 0-7513-1086-7

CONTENTS

PREFACE

This Thai Phrase Book has the same excellent pedigree as others in the Hugo series, having been compiled by experts to meet the general needs of tourists and business travellers, but it is – as you might expect – a little different. Arranged under the usual headings of 'Hotels', 'Shopping' and so forth, an ample selection of useful words and phrases is shown with an easy-to-follow system of imitated pronunciation sandwiched between the English and Thai characters. Although plenty of guidance is given regarding pronunciation (see pages 5-6), there are – as in Chinese – some tricky tones to master; if you feel unsure of yourself, simply point to the phrase you want to say.

Of course you will want to know what various signs and notices mean when they are written in Thai characters; there are lists of common signs (page 14) and road signs (pages 31-32), as well as recognition boxes headed *Things you'll see* in most sections of the book. These cover words, signs, notices etc; the Thai script is given alongside its pronunciation and the English translation.

A 1200-line Mini-Dictionary will help you form additional phrases (or at least express the one word you need!), and the extensive Menu Reader will ease your way through complicated Thai meals. Under the heading *Cross-cultural Notes* you will find guidance on aspects of the Thai way of life – points of etiquette, good manners and customs. An understanding of such matters will greatly enhance your trip to Thailand, and your hosts will appreciate all the effort you have made to respect their culture and to speak their language.

PRONUNCIATION

When reading the imitated pronunciation, pronounce each syllable as if it formed part of an English word and you will be understood sufficiently well. Remember the points below and your pronunciation will be even closer to the correct Thai. Use our audio cassette of selected extracts from this book, and you should be word-perfect!

a	as in 'ago'
e	as in 'hen'
i	as in 'thin'
o	as in 'on'
u	as in 'gun'
ah	as in 'rather'
ai	as in 'Thai'
air	as in 'pair'
ao	as in 'Mao Tse-Tung'
ay	as in 'day'
ee	as in 'see'
er	as in 'enter'
er-ee	(don't pronounce the 'r')
eu	as in a sound of disgust which a comic might write as 'errgh'
ew	as in 'few'
oh	as in 'go'
oo	as in 'boot'
oo	as in 'book'
oy	as in 'toy'
bp	between a 'b' and a 'p' – not a double sound
dt	between a 'd' and a 't' – not a double sound
g	as in 'give'
j	as in 'jet'
ng	as in 'sing'

When 'p', 't' and 'k' sounds occur at the end of words in Thai, the sound is 'swallowed' or 'not released'.

Note that many Thais have difficulty in pronouncing 'r' sounds and will substitute an 'l'; thus a-rai ('what?') often becomes a-lai.

TONES

Thai is a tonal language. This means that the pitch at which a syllable is pronounced determines its meaning. Thus, the word 'mâi', pronounced with a falling intonation means 'not' but the word 'mǎi', pronounced with a rising intonation, means 'silk'.

There are five tones in Thai:

mid tone	no symbol
falling tone	ˆ
rising tone	ˇ
high tone	´
low tone	`

Mid-tone: this is similar to the normal pitch of voice.

Falling tone: this can be thought of as similar to an emphatic pronunciation in English, as for example, when repeating a word a number of times over the telephone.

Rising tone: this is rather like a questioning intonation.

High tone: this is pitched slightly higher than normal.

Low tone: this is pitched slightly lower than normal.

MALE/FEMALE

The forms kâ, dee-chún and chún given in brackets replace the preceding word and are used by female speakers. For example, kOOn krúp (ka): kOOn krúp is used by a man and kOOn kâ by a woman.

CROSS-CULTURAL NOTES

Visitors to Thailand are always impressed by the warmth, friendliness and tolerance of Thai people. Nevertheless, there are certain important dos and don'ts which the visitor should observe so as not to cause offence.

* the monarchy

The monarchy is highly revered in Thailand. Criticism of the institution or members of the royal family, whether real or imagined, is deeply offensive to most Thais and can lead to serious trouble. Few Thais would wish to seriously discuss anything to do with the monarchy with a foreign visitor, and these feelings should be respected.

* religion

Buddhism likewise is regarded as an essential part of 'Thainess'. Temples, Buddha images and monks should all be treated with appropriate respect; shoes should be removed in certain parts of the temple and any restrictions on taking photographs should be observed. Monks are strictly forbidden to have any physical contact with women, so female visitors in particular should make certain that they do not accidentally come into close contact with a monk; on buses, for example, where it is normal to give up one's seat to a monk, women will consciously avoid sitting next to them.

* appearances

In Thailand people are judged very much by their appearance and most Thais invest considerable time, effort and money in order to look good. As a result they cannot help but look askance at the sometimes rather sloppily attired western visitors they see; while they will generally be much too polite to say what they think directly, the warning notices in many temples refusing admission to unacceptably dressed visitors reflect the disapproval that Thais instinctively feel. So if you are meeting Thai friends or visiting them at their homes it is only good manners to go to the effort of looking respectable, even if this means erring on the conservative side in your style of dress.

★ meeting Thais

You should address Thais who are of similar age or older than yourself by using the polite title 'khun' in front of their first name, regardless of whether you are speaking to a man or a woman. Thus Mr Somchai Sombatcharoen would be addressed (and referred to) as *Khun Somchai* and Mrs Nuantip Bunsin as *Khun Nuantip*.

If you are invited to a Thai home remember to take your shoes off just before entering the house. Members of the household will probably greet you with a 'wai' – a gesture of both greeting and respect in which the hands are held together in a prayer-like attitude in front of the face – which should be returned. The fingertips should be nearer the forehead when 'wai-ing' people of equal or superior status and nearer the chin when responding to the 'wai' of children or those of inferior status. Thais also show respect to older or more senior people by trying to keep their head at a lower level when passing by them or talking to them; while this custom does not have to be observed too literally, it is, for example, a mark of good manners to make an obvious gesture of bending forward a little when passing elderly members of the household who might be seated.

When Thais meet casually or by chance, they will often greet each other with the question 'bpai nǎi?' (where are you going?) or 'bpai nǎi mah?' (where have you been?). This is usually more an informal greeting than an attempt to find out about their friend's immediate destination or recent whereabouts, and a rather vague answer, such as 'bpai têe-o' (I'm going out) or 'bpai têe-o mah' (I've been out) is a perfectly acceptable response.

★ surface harmony

In Thailand the preservation of surface harmony is considered of the utmost importance. Losing one's temper, arguing and direct criticism of others are regarded as threats to such harmony and consequently frowned upon.

* personal conduct

Westerners can unintentionally cause offence by pointing at things with their foot, sitting in such a way that their feet are pointing at a Thai and by touching or patting Thais on the head. Such actions will cause Thais considerable discomfort even if they are too polite to say as much. Many of Bangkok's long-suffering samlor drivers sit silently fuming while thoughtless tourists rest their feet on the rail behind the driver's seat, only inches from his head.

Displaying physical affection in public towards a member of the opposite sex is also frowned upon by many Thais, although in recent years it has become more common to see young couples in Bangkok holding hands. Physical contact between friends of the same sex, however, is perfectly acceptable and it is not uncommon to see young men or young women walking hand in hand with a friend of the same sex.

* polite language

An important way of expressing politeness when speaking Thai is to use a polite particle – a word for which there is no equivalent in English – at the end of a sentence. Thus, men will add the word 'krúp' at the end of both statements and questions in order to sound more polite, while women will say 'ká' at the end of questions and 'kâ' at the end of statements. While these particles have generally been omitted in the phrases given in this book you are advised to add them on to the end of every phrase at first, on the grounds that it is generally better to sound too polite than not polite enough; gradually you will learn when it is unnecessary to use them.

USEFUL EVERYDAY PHRASES

Yes/no
châi/mâi châi
ใช่/ไม่ใช่
or
krúp (kâ)/mâi krúp (kâ)
ครับ (คะ) / ไม่ครับ (คะ)

There is no single word for 'yes' and 'no' in Thai, the appropriate word depending on the way in which the question is phrased. Generally, to answer 'yes' to a question, the verb in the question is repeated; and to say 'no', the negative word **'mâi'** is used in front of the verb (for an example, see page 51). Since questions are often phrased in the form of a statement followed by '**... châi mái?**' (isn't that so?) the word **'châi'** is often thought of as being equivalent to 'yes' and **'mâi châi'** equivalent to 'no'. In addition, the polite particles **'krúp'** (spoken by men) and **'kâ'** (spoken by women) are also used to mean 'yes' and **'mâi krúp (kâ)'** to mean 'no'.

Thank you/No thank you
kòrp-kOOn/mâi ao kòrp-kOOn
ขอบคุณ / ไม่เอาขอบคุณ

Please (*offering*)
chern krúp (kâ)
เชิญครับ (คะ)

Please (*asking for something*)
kǒr ...
ขอ...

Please (*asking someone to do something*)
chôo-ay ...
ช่วย ...

I don't understand
mâi kâo-jai
ไม่เข้าใจ

Do you speak English?
pôot pah-săh ung-grìt bpen mái?
พูดภาษาอังกฤษเป็นไหม

I can't speak Thai
pôot pah-săh tai mâi bpen
พูดภาษาไทยไม่เป็น

I don't know
mâi sâhp
ไม่ทราบ

Please speak more slowly
chôo-ay pôot cháh cháh nòy dâi mái
ช่วยพูดช้า ๆ หน่อยได้ไหม

Please write it down for me
chôo-ay kĕe-un long hâi nòy dâi mái?
ช่วยเขียนลงให้หน่อยได้ไหม

My name is ...
pŏm (dee-chún) chêu ...
ผม (ดิฉัน) ชื่อ ...

How do you do, pleased to meet you
sa-wùt dee krúp (kâ), yin dee têe dâi róo-jùk
สวัสดีครับ (ค่ะ) ยินดีที่ได้รู้จัก

Good morning/afternoon/evening
sa-wùt dee krúp (kâ)
สวัสดีครับ (ค่ะ)

Goodbye
lah gòrn ná
ลาก่อนนะ

How are you?
bpen yung-ngai bâhng?
เป็นอย่างไรบ้าง

Excuse me please
kŏr-tôht krúp (kâ)
ขอโทษครับ (คะ)

Sorry!
kŏr-tôht krúp (kâ)
ขอโทษครับ (คะ)

I'm really sorry
pŏm (dee-chún) sĕe-a jai jing jing
ผม (ดิฉัน) เสียใจจริง ๆ

Can you help me?
chôo-ay pŏm (dee-chún) nòy dâi mái?
ช่วยผม (ดิฉัน) หน่อยได้ไหม

Can I have ...?
kŏr ...
ขอ ...

I would like ...
ao ...
เอา ...

Is there ... here?
têe-nêe mee ... mái?
ที่นี่มี ...ไหม

Where can I get …?
séu … dâi têe-năi?
ซื้อ … ได้ที่ไหน

How much is it?
tâo-rài krúp (ká)?
เท่าไรครับ (คะ)

What time is it?
gèe mohng láir-o?
กี่โมงแล้ว

I must go now
dtôrng bpai la
ต้องไปละ

I've lost my way
pŏm (dee-chún) lŏng tahng
ผม (ดิฉัน) หลงทาง

Do you take credit cards?
têe-nêe rúp bùt kray-dìt mái?
ที่นี่รับบัตรเครดิตไหม

Where is the toilet?
hôrng náhm yòo têe-năi?
ห้องน้ำอยู่ที่ไหน

Go away!
bpai hâi pón
ไปให้พ้น

Excellent!
yêe-um ler-ee
เยี่ยมเลย

THINGS YOU'LL SEE

ปิด	bpìt	closed
ไม่ว่าง	mâi wâhng	engaged
ให้เช่า	hâi châo	for rent
ขาย	kăi	for sale
สุภาพบุรุษ	soo-pâhp boo-ròot	gentlemen
หญิง	yĭng	ladies
ญ.		ladies
สุภาพสตรี	soo-pâhp sa-dtree	ladies
ลิฟท์	líf	lift
ชาย	chai	men
ช.		men
ห้ามเข้า	hâhm kâo	no admittance
ห้ามสูบบุหรี่	hâhm sòop boo-rèe	no smoking
เปิด	bpèrt	open
เปิดเวลา	bpèrt way-lah	opening times
ดึง	deung	pull
ผลัก	plùk	push
ลดราคา	lót rah-kah	sale
เงียบ	ngêe-up	silence/quiet
สุขา	sòo-kăh	toilets
ห้องน้ำ	hôrng náhm	toilets
ทางเข้า	tahng kâo	way in
ทางออก	tahng òrk	way out

THINGS YOU'LL HEAR

a-rai ná?	Pardon?
bpen yung-ngai bâhng?	How are you?
dĕe-o póp gun mài	See you later
kòrp-kOOn	Thanks
kŏr-tôht	Excuse me
mâi bpen rai	You're welcome/never mind
mâi kâo jai	I don't understand
mâi sâhp/róo	I don't know
nêe ngai lâ	Here you are
ra-wung !	Look out!
rĕu krúp (ká)?	Is that so?
sa-bai dee krúp (kâ) – láir-o kOOn lâ	Very well, thank you – and you?
sa-wùt dee krúp (kâ)	Goodbye
sa-wùt dee krúp (kâ) yin dee têe dâi róo-jùk gun	How do you do, nice to meet you
tòok láir-o	That's right

15

DAYS, MONTHS, SEASONS

Sunday	wun ah-tít	วันอาทิตย์
Monday	wun jun	วันจันทร์
Tuesday	wun ung-kahn	วันอังคาร
Wednesday	wun pÓOt	วันพุธ
Thursday	wun pa-réu-hùt	วันพฤหัส
Friday	wun sÒOk	วันศุกร์
Saturday	wun săo	วันเสาร์

January	mók-ga-rah-kom	มกราคม
February	gOOm-pah-pun	กุมภาพันธ์
March	mee-nah-kom	มีนาคม
April	may-săh-yon	เมษายน
May	préut-sa-pah-kom	พฤษภาคม
June	mí-tOO-nah-yon	มิถุนายน
July	ga-rúk-ga-dah-kom	กรกฎาคม
August	sĭng-hăh-kom	สิงหาคม
September	gun-yah-yon	กันยายน
October	dtOO-lah-kom	ตุลาคม
November	préut-sa-jik-gah-yon	พฤศจิกายน
December	tun-wah-kom	ธันวาคม

Spring	réu-doo bai-mái plì	ฤดูใบไม้ผลิ
Summer	réu-doo rórn	ฤดูร้อน
Autumn	réu-doo bai-mái rôo-ung	ฤดูใบไม้ร่วง
Winter	réu-doo năo	ฤดูหนาว

cool season (Nov-Feb)	nâh năo	หน้าหนาว
hot season (Mar-June)	nâh rórn	หน้าร้อน
rainy season (Jul-Oct)	nâh fŏn	หน้าฝน
Christmas	krít-sa-maht	คริสต์มาส
New Year	bpee mài	ปีใหม่
New Year's Eve	wun sîn bpee	วันสิ้นปี
Thai New Year (April)	sŏng-grahn	สงกรานต์
Chinese New Year	dtròot jeen	ตรุษจีน

NUMBERS, COUNTING

In the Thai script the first item is the numeral and the second the word.

0	sǒon	๐	ศูนย์
1	nèung	๑	หนึ่ง
2	sǒrng	๒	สอง
3	sǎhm	๓	สาม
4	sèe	๔	สี่
5	hâh	๕	ห้า
6	hòk	๖	หก
7	jèt	๗	เจ็ด
8	bpàirt	๘	แปด
9	gâo	๙	เก้า
10	sìp	๑๐	สิบ
11	sìp-èt	๑๑	สิบเอ็ด
12	sìp-sǒrng	๑๒	สิบสอง
13	sìp-sǎhm	๑๓	สิบสาม
14	sìp-sèe	๑๔	สิบสี่
15	sìp-hâh	๑๕	สิบห้า
16	sìp-hòk	๑๖	สิบหก
17	sìp-jèt	๑๗	สิบเจ็ด
18	sìp-bpàirt	๑๘	สิบแปด
19	sìp-gâo	๑๙	สิบเก้า
20	yêe-sìp	๒๐	ยี่สิบ
21	yêe-sìp-èt	๒๑	ยี่สิบเอ็ด

22 yêe-sìp-sŏrng	๒๒	ยี่สิบสอง
30 săhm-sìp	๓๐	สามสิบ
31 săhm-sìp-èt	๓๑	สามสิบเอ็ด
32 săhm-sìp sŏrng	๓๒	สามสิบสอง
40 sèe-sìp	๔๐	สี่สิบ
50 hâh-sìp	๕๐	ห้าสิบ
60 hòk-sìp	๖๐	หกสิบ
70 jèt-sìp	๗๐	เจ็ดสิบ
80 bpàirt-sìp	๘๐	แปดสิบ
90 gâo-sìp	๙๐	เก้าสิบ
100 nèung róy	๑๐๐	หนึ่งร้อย
101 nèung róy nèung	๑๐๑	หนึ่งร้อยหนึ่ง
110 nèung róy sìp	๑๑๐	หนึ่งร้อยสิบ
200 sŏrng róy	๒๐๐	สองร้อย
300 săhm róy	๓๐๐	สามร้อย
400 sèe róy	๔๐๐	สี่ร้อย
1000 nèung pun	๑๐๐๐	หนึ่งพัน
10,000 nèung mèun	๑๐๐๐๐	หนึ่งหมื่น
20,000 sŏrng mèun	๒๐๐๐๐	สองหมื่น
100,000 nèung săirn	๑๐๐๐๐๐	หนึ่งแสน
1,000,000 nèung láhn	๑๐๐๐๐๐๐	หนึ่งล้าน

COUNTING

When using number words with nouns Thai also uses *classifiers*. Sometimes these are similar to English, for example (note the word order):

two bowls of egg noodles   **three bottles of beer**
ba-mèe sŏrng chahm   bee-a săhm kòo-ut
(egg noodles – two – bowls) **(beer – three – bottles)**

The words 'bowls' and 'bottles' in these phrases act like classifiers in Thai. But whereas English uses these classifier-like words only in certain cases, Thai always needs a classifier with a noun:

three tickets
dtŏo-a săhm bai
(ticket – three – classifier for tickets)

two cars
rót sŏrng kun
(car – two – classifier for vehicles)

The words 'bai' and 'kun' in these examples are classifiers which have no equivalent in the English translations.

The counting word comes before the classifier unless only one object is being referred to, in which case the word for 'one' comes after the classifier:

one/a coffee
gah-fair tôo-ay nèung
(coffee – cup – one)

one/a friend
pêu-un kon nèung
(friend – classifier – one)

The most common classifiers are:

kon	people (other than monks and royalty)
kun	vehicles
cha-bùp	letters, newspapers, documents
chín	pieces of things, such as cake, meat, cloth etc
dtoo-a	animals
bai	fruit, eggs, leaves, items of crockery, slips of paper
lêm	books, knives
lǔng	houses
lôok	fruit, balls
hôrng	rooms
hàirng	places
un	things – a general classifier that can be used for counting inanimate things when you can't remember the correct classifier.

The words for various units of time and measure behave like classifiers:

three days
sǎhm wun

five kilometres
hâh gi-loh-mét

one year
bpee nèung

one kilo
gi-loh nèung

TIME, THE CALENDAR

today	wun née	วันนี้
yesterday	mêu-a wahn née	เมื่อวานนี้
tomorrow	prôong née	พรุ่งนี้
the day before yesterday	wun seun née	วันซืนนี้
the day after tomorrow	wun ma-reun née	วันมะรืนนี้
this week	ah-tít née	อาทิตย์นี้
last week	ah-tít gòrn	อาทิตย์ก่อน
next week	ah-tít nâh	อาทิตย์หน้า
this morning	cháo née	เช้านี้
this afternoon	bài née	บ่ายนี้
this evening	yen née	เย็นนี้
tonight	keun née	คืนนี้
yesterday afternoon	bài wahn née	บ่ายวานนี้
last night	mêu-a keun née	เมื่อคืนนี้
tomorrow morning	prôong née cháo	พรุ่งนี้เช้า
tomorrow night	prôong née glahng keun	พรุ่งนี้กลางคืน
in three days	èek sǎhm wun	อีกสามวัน
three days ago	sǎhm wun gòrn	สามวันก่อน
late	cháh	ช้า
early	ray-o	เร็ว

22

soon	nai mâi cháh	ในไม่ช้า
later on	tee lǔng	ทีหลัง
at the moment	děe-o née	เดี๋ยวนี้
second	wí-nah-tee	วินาที
minute	nah-tee	นาที
one minute	nèung nah-tee	หนึ่งนาที
two minutes	sǒrng nah-tee	สองนาที
quarter of an hour	sìp-hâh nah-tee	สิบห้านาที
half an hour	krêung chôo-a mohng	ครึ่งชั่วโมง
three quarters of an hour	sèe sìp-hâh nah-tee	สี่สิบห้านาที
hour	chôo-a mohng	ชั่วโมง
that day	wun nún	วันนั้น
every day	tóok wun	ทุกวัน
all day	túng wun	ทั้งวัน
the next day	wun rôong kêun	วันรุ่งขึ้น

TELLING THE TIME

midnight	tê-ung keun	**midday**	tê-ung wun
1 a.m.	dtee nèung	**1 p.m.**	bài mohng
2 a.m.	dtee sǒrng	**2 p.m.**	bài sǒrng mohng
3 a.m.	dtee sǎhm	**3 p.m.**	bài sǎhm mohng
4 a.m.	dtee sèe	**4 p.m.**	bài sèe mohng
5 a.m.	dtee hâh	**5 p.m.**	hâh mohng yen
6 a.m.	hòk mohng cháo	**6 p.m.**	hòk mohng yen
7 a.m.	jèt mohng cháo	**7 p.m.**	tôom nèung
or	mohng cháo		
8 a.m.	sǒrng mohng cháo	**8 p.m.**	sǒrng tôom

23

9 a.m.	săhm mohng cháo	**9 p.m.**	săhm tôom
10 a.m.	sèe mohng cháo	**10 p.m.**	sèe tôom
11 a.m.	hâh mohng cháo	**11 p.m.**	hâh tôom

The word for 'half' is 'krêung' which is added to the hour; minutes past the hour are expressed in the form: hour – number of minutes – **'nah-tee'** (minute), while minutes to the hour are expressed as **'èek'** (further) – number of minutes – **nah-tee** – hour. There is no special word for 'quarter' past/to in Thai. The twenty-four hour clock system is used in formal announcements such as on radio; the word **'nah-li-gah'** is used for 'hours' and **'nah-tee'** for 'minutes'.

1.10 p.m.	bài mohng sìp nah-tee
1.15 p.m.	bài mohng sìp-hâh nah-tee
1.30 p.m.	bài mohng krêung
1.40 p.m.	èek yêe-sìp nah-tee bài sŏrng mohng
1.45 p.m.	èek sìp-hâh nah-tee bài sŏrng mohng
19.00 hrs	sìp-gâo nah-li-gah
20. 30 hrs	yêe-sìp nah-li-gah săhm sìp nah-tee

THE CALENDAR

The date is expressed by the pattern:

wun *(day)* + têe + *number* + *month*

wun têe nèung mee-nah-kom	1st March
wun têe sìp-hâh may-săh-yon	15th April

In Thailand the year is normally given according to the Buddhist Era. This is calculated by adding 543 to the A.D. year. So 1990 A.D. = 2533 (B.E.).

HOTELS

With tourism playing a major role in the Thai economy it is not surprising that Bangkok offers the traveller a wide variety of accommodation ranging from cheap guest houses to luxurious hotels. Outside Bangkok, hotels are readily found in all provincial capitals and major towns; while those towns involved in international tourism will offer the most luxurious facilities, more modest yet comfortable accommodation is available at a very reasonable price.

In the larger Bangkok hotels, all of the staff will be able to speak English, while some will have spent some years abroad. Since using English is an important part of their job, it would be quite inappropriate to attempt to carry out transactions in Thai unless you are a very fluent speaker of the language. Outside Bangkok, some knowledge of Thai, especially in the less-visited provinces, is both useful and appreciated.

Nearly all hotel rooms in Bangkok are air-conditioned, but up-country, an electric ceiling fan is a common alternative. All rooms will have a bathroom included, consisting of a wash-basin, western-style (usually) toilet and either a bath tub or a large water jar for Thai-style bathing.

Thais use the English term 'single room' to refer to a room with a double bed and 'double room' to mean a room with two single beds; so be prepared for misunderstandings!

Meals are not included as part of the hotel charge; often the hotel will have its own coffee shop where both Thai and western food can be ordered, while international standard hotels have their own restaurants.

'Hotel' is traditionally a rather ambiguous term in Thai: many cheap 'hotels' are brothels, while many slightly more respectable-looking premises are used primarily for fleeting amorous encounters. If in doubt, consult a guide book, the Thai Tourist Organisation or simply ask a Thai whether it is a suitable place to stay.

USEFUL WORDS AND PHRASES

air-conditioner	krêu-ung air	เครื่องแอร์
air-conditioned room	hôrng air	ห้องแอร์
bedroom	hôrng norn	ห้องนอน
bill	bin	บิล
breakfast	ah-hăhn cháo	อาหารเช้า
coffee shop	kórp-fêe chórp	คอฟฟี่ช้อป
double room	hôrng kôo	ห้องคู่
fan	pút lom	พัดลม
hotel	rohng-rairm	โรงแรม
key	gOOn-jair	กุญแจ
manager	pôo-jùt-gahn	ผู้จัดการ
room	hôrng	ห้อง
shower	fùk boo-a	ฝักบัว
single room	hôrng dèe-o	ห้องเดี่ยว
swimming pool	sà wâi náhm	สระว่ายน้ำ
toilet	hôrng náhm	ห้องน้ำ
twin room	hôrng kôo	ห้องคู่
window screen (*against mosquitos*)	mÓOng lôo-ut	มุ้งลวด

Have you any vacancies?
mee hôrng wâhng mái?
มีห้องว่างไหม

I have a reservation
pŏm(dee-chún) jorng hôrng wái láir-o
ผม (ดิฉัน) จองห้องไว้แล้ว

I'd like a single/double room with air-conditioning
ao hôrng dèe-o/hôrng kôo dtìt air
เอาห้องเดี่ยว/ห้องคู่ติดแอร์

What is the charge per night?
kâh hôrng wun la tâo-rài?
ค่าห้องวันละเท่าไร

I'd like a room for one night/three nights
pŏm (dee-chún) ja púk yòo keun nèung/săhm keun
ผม (ดิฉัน) จะพักอยู่คืนหนึ่ง / สามคืน

Does the room have air-conditioning?
hôrng dtìt air rĕu bplào?
ห้องติดแอร์หรือเปล่า

I don't know yet how long I'll stay
mâi sâhp wâh ja yòo nahn tâo-rài
ไม่ทราบว่าจะอยู่นานเท่าไร

Can I see the room first please?
kŏr doo hôrng gòrn dâi mái?
ขอดูห้องก่อนได้ไหม

Can you spray some mosquito repellent please?
chôo-ay chèet yah gun yOong hâi nòy dâi mái?
ช่วยฉีดยากันยุงให้หน่อยได้ไหม

Would you have my luggage brought up?
chôo-ay yók gra-bpăo mah hâi nòy dâi mái?
ช่วยยกกระเป๋ามาให้หน่อยได้ไหม

Can I have a bottle of drinking water, please?
kŏr náhm gin kòo-ut nèung dâi mái?
ขอน้ำกินขวดหนึ่งได้ไหม

Please call me at ... o'clock
chôo-ay rêe-uk pŏm (dee-chún) way-lah ... mohng
ช่วยเรียกผม (ดิฉัน) เวลา ...โมง

I'll be back at ... o'clock
pŏm (dee-chún) ja glùp way-lah ... mohng
ผม (ดิฉัน) จะกลับเวลา ...โมง

Can I leave some things in the safe?
kŏr fàhk kŏrng wái nai dtôo sáyf dâi mái?
ขอฝากของไว้ในตู้เซฟได้ไหม

My room number is ...
pŏm (dee-chún) yòo hôrng ber ...
ผมดิฉันอยู่ห้องเบอร์ ...

I'm leaving tomorrow
pŏm (dee-chún) ja bpai prôong-née
ผม (ดิฉัน) จะไปพรุ่งนี้

Can I have the bill please?
kŏr bin nòy dâi mái?
ขอบิลหน่อยได้ไหม

Can you get me a taxi?
chôo-ay rêe-uk táirk-sêe hâi nòy dâi mái?
ช่วยเรียกแท็กซี่ให้หน่อยได้ไหม

THINGS YOU'LL SEE

คอฟฟี่ช้อป	kórp-fêe chórp	coffee shop
สอบถาม	sòrp tăhm	enquiries
ทางออก	tahng òrk	exit →

ชั้น	chún	floor
สุภาพบุรุษ	soo-pâhp boo-ròot	gentlemen
หญิง	yǐng	ladies
สุภาพสตรี	soo-pâhp sa-dtree	ladies
ลิฟท์	lif	lift
บริการรถรับส่ง	bor-ri-gahn rót rúp sòng	limousine service
ชาย	chai	men
ห้ามสูบบุหรี่	hâhm sòop boo-rèe	no smoking
แผนกต้อนรับ	pa-nàirk dtôrn rúp	reception
บริการนำเที่ยว	bor-ri-gahn num têe-o	sight-seeing tours
ห้องน้ำ	hôrng náhm	toilet
ยินดีต้อนรับ	yin dee dtôrn rúp	welcome

MOTORING

Bangkok's reputation as one of the world's worst traffic spots is well-deserved. With far too many cars per kilometre and a driving culture in which traffic regulations are viewed as inconveniences to be circumvented, driving in the capital itself is tiring and stressful. In theory, people drive on the left; in practice, cars tend to overtake on all sides, with cheerful disregard to lane discipline and rights of way, while motorcyclists perform kamikaze stunts cutting across and through speeding traffic with inches to spare. A further complication is that in the ceaseless search for a solution to Bangkok's traffic problems new restrictions – such as declaring certain routes one-way only during the rush hour – are often introduced at short notice.

Driving up-country involves different hazards. There is a good network of roads linking the provinces and a constant flow of lorries and buses carrying goods and passengers back and forth. The roads, however, are generally narrow, with little room for evasive action if the driver of an oncoming vehicle dozes off at the wheel; an often casual attitude to the need for headlights when driving at night – both on inter-provincial highways and within provincial towns – should deter the visitor from night-driving except in emergencies.

If you do decide to drive in Thailand, you will need nerves of steel and an international driving licence. You will find car-hire companies advertised in the local English-language newspapers. Since Thai motorists are seldom insured, parties in an accident generally negotiate – sometimes heatedly – on the spot about responsibility and payment for damage. If agreement cannot be reached amicably, the police are often called in to mediate. In any such negotiations, the foreigner is somewhat at a disadvantage.

Thailand offers an ideal climate for motorcycling, and touring in the provinces can seem a very attractive and practical way of seeing the country. All too many visitors, unfortunately, through a combination of over-enthusiasm, inexperience, and poorly-maintained machines, find it a rather costlier and more painful venture than they had originally anticipated. Unless you are an experienced rider and have sufficient mechanical know-how to judge whether the bike you are hiring is in a roadworthy condition, then motorbikes are probably best left well alone.

SOME COMMON ROAD SIGNS

40 ก.ม.	sèe sìp gi-loh-mét	40 kilometres
3 ม.	săhm mét	3 metres
4 ตัน	sèe dtun	4 tons
ทางโค้ง	tahng kóhng	bend
ระวัง	ra-wung	caution
อันตราย	un-dta-rai	danger
ทางเบี่ยง	tahng bèe-ung	diversion
ขับช้า ๆ	kùp cháh cháh	drive slowly
หยุด	yòot	halt
หยุด – ตรวจ	yòot -dtròo-ut	halt – checkpoint
โรงพยาบาล	rohng pa-yah-bahn	hospital – no
ห้ามใช้เสียง	hâhm chái sĕe-ung	sounding horn
ชิดซ้าย	chít sái	keep to the left
ห้ามเข้า	hâhm kâo	no entry
ห้ามแซง	hâhm sairng	no overtaking
ห้ามจอด	hâhm jòrt	no parking
ห้ามเลี้ยว	hâhm lée-o	no turning
ห้ามกลับรถ	hâhm glùp rót	no U-turns
ห้ามรถทุกชนิด	hâhm rót tóok cha-nít	no vehicles

→

ทางรถไฟ	tahng rót fai	railway
โรงเรียน	rohng ree-un	school

USEFUL WORDS AND PHRASES

automatic ùt-ta-noh-mút   อัตโนมัติ
boot gra-bprohng tái rót   กระโปรงท้ายรถ
breakdown rót sěe-a   รถเสีย
brake (noun) bràyk   เบรค
car rót   รถ
clutch klút   คลัทช์
crossroads sèe yâirk   สี่แยก
to drive kùp   ขับ
engine krêu-ung yon   เครื่องยนต์
exhaust tôr ai sěe-a   ท่อไอเสีย
fanbelt sǎi pahn   สายพาน
garage (for repairs) òo sôrm rót   อู่ซ่อมรถ
  (for petrol) bpúm núm mun   ปั๊มน้ำมัน
gear gee-a   เกียร์
junction (on motorway) tahng yâirk   ทางแยก
licence bai kùp kèe   ใบขับขี่
lights (head) fai nâh rót   ไฟหน้ารถ
  (rear) fai lǔng rót   ไฟหลังรถ
lorry rót bun-tóok   รถบรรทุก
manual gee-a meu   เกียร์มือ

mirror	gra-jòk	กระจก
motorbike	rót mor-dter-sai	รถมอเตอร์ไซค์
motorway	tahng dòo-un	ทางด่วน
number plate	pàirn bpâi ber rót	แผ่นป้ายเบอร์รถ
petrol	núm mun	น้ำมัน
road	ta-nǒn	ถนน
to skid	cha-làirp	แฉลบ
spares	krêu-ung a-lài	เครื่องอะไหล่
speed *(noun)*	kwahm ray-o	ความเร็ว
speed limit	ùt-dtrah kwahm ray-o	อัตราความเร็ว
speedometer	krêu-ung wút kwahm ray-o	เครื่องวัดความเร็ว
steering wheel	poo-ung mah-lai	พวงมาลัย
to tow	lâhk	ลาก
traffic	ja-rah-jorn	จราจร
traffic jam	rót dtìt	รถติด
traffic lights	fai sǔn-yahn ja-rah-jorn	ไฟสัญญาณจราจร
tyre	yahng rót	ยางรถ
van	rót dtôo	รถตู้
wheel	lór	ล้อ
windscreen	gra-jòk nâh rót	กระจกหน้ารถ
windscreen wipers	têe bpùt núm fǒn	ที่ปัดน้ำฝน

I'd like some petrol/oil/water
dtôrng-gahn núm mun/núm mun krêu-ung/náhm
ต้องการน้ำมัน / น้ำมันเครื่อง / น้ำ

Fill her up please!
dterm núm mun hâi dtem
เติมน้ำมันให้เต็ม

I'd like 10 litres of petrol
dtôrng-gahn núm mun sìp lít
ต้องการน้ำมันสิบลิตร

Would you check the tyres please?
chôo-ay dtròo-ut yahng hâi nòy dâi mái?
ช่วยตรวจยางให้หน่อยได้ไหม

Do you do repairs here?
têe-nêe sôrm rót dâi mái?
ที่นี่ซ่อมรถได้ไหม

Can you repair the clutch?
ja sôrm klút hâi nòy dâi mái?
จะซ่อมคลัทช์ให้หน่อยได้ไหม

How long will it take?
ja chai way-lah nahn tâo-rài?
จะใช้เวลานานเท่าไร

Where can I park?
jòrt dâi têe-nǎi?
จอดได้ที่ไหน

Can I park here?
jòrt têe-nêe dâi mái?
จอดที่นี่ได้ไหม

There is something wrong with the brakes
bràyk mâi kôy dee
เบรคไม่ค่อยดี

The engine is overheating
krêu-ung yon rórn

เครื่องยนตร์ร้อน

I need a new tyre
dtôrng-gahn yahng mài

ต้องการยางใหม่

I'd like to hire a car
yàhk ja châo rót

อยากจะเช่ารถ

Where is the nearest garage?
mee òo sôrm rót yòo têe-năi?

มีอู่ซ่อมรถอยู่ที่ไหน

How do I get to …?
bpai … bpai tahng năi?

ไป … ไปทางไหน

Is this the road to …?
nêe ta-nŏn bpai … châi mái?

นี่ถนนไป …ใช่ไหม

DIRECTIONS YOU MAY BE GIVEN

ler-ee bpai èek
straight on

yòo tahng sái
on the left

→

---

lée-o sái
turn left

yòo tahng kwăh
on the right

lée-o kwăh
turn right

lée-o kwăh tahng yâirk têe nèung
first on the right

lée-o sái tahng yâirk têe sŏrng
second on the left

ler-ee ... bpai
past the ...

THINGS YOU'LL SEE

บริการ 24 ช.ม.	bor-ri-gahn yêe-sìp sèe chôo-a mohng	24 hour service
อู่	òo	garage
ห้ามสูบบุหรี่	hâhm sòop bOO-rèe	no smoking
ปะยาง	bpà yahng	punctures repaired
บริการซ่อมรถ	bor-ri-gahn sôrm rót	repair service
อะไหล่	a-lài	spares

RAIL TRAVEL

Travelling up-country by train in Thailand is usually slower than travelling by bus. The Thai railway network consists of four major routes linking Bangkok to the north, the south, the lower north-east and the upper north-east. Three types of train operate along these routes: the slow, ordinary trains, the optimistically-called 'rapid' trains and 'express' trains which are the fastest. Train reservations can be made at Bangkok's Hua Lampong Station and for long-distance journeys sleeping cars can be booked.

USEFUL WORDS AND PHRASES

booking office   têe jorng dtŏo-a — ที่จองตั๋ว
carriage   dtôo — ตู้
connection   dtòr rót — ต่อรถ
engine   krêu-ung jùk — เครื่องจักร
first class   chún nèung — ชั้นหนึ่ง
to get in   kêun — ขึ้น
to get out   long — ลง
guard   pa-núk ngahn fâo dtròo-ut — พนักงานเฝ้าตรวจ
left luggage office   têe fâhk — ที่ฝากกระเป๋า
    gra-bpǎo
lost property   têe jâirng kŏrng hǎi — ที่แจ้งของหาย
luggage trolley   têe lâhk — ที่ลากกระเป๋า
    gra-bpǎo
platform   chahn chah-lah — ชานชาลา
rail   rahng rót — รางรถ
railway   tahng rót fai — ทางรถไฟ
reserved seat   jorng láir-o — จองแล้ว

return ticket dtŏo-a bpai glùp   ตั๋วไปกลับ

seat têe nûng   ที่นั่ง

second class chún sŏrng   ชั้นสอง

single ticket dtŏo-a bpai tahng dee-o   ตั๋วไปทางเดียว

sleeping car rót norn   รถนอน

station sa-tăhn-nee rót fai   สถานีรถไฟ

ticket dtŏo-a   ตั๋ว

ticket office têe jum-nài dtŏo-a   ที่จำหน่ายตั๋ว

timetable dtah-rahng way-lah   ตารางเวลา

train rót fai   รถไฟ

waiting room hôrng púk   ห้องพัก

window nâh dtàhng   หน้าต่าง

When does the train for ... leave?
rót fai bpai ... òrk gèe mohng?
รถไฟไป ... ออกกี่โมง

When does the train from ... arrive?
rót fai jàhk ... tĕung gèe mohng?
รถไฟจาก ... ถึงกี่โมง

When is the next train to ...?
rót fai bpai ... ka-boo-un nâh òrk gèe mohng?
รถไฟไป ... ขบวนหน้าออกกี่โมง

When is the first train to ...?
rót fai bpai ... ka-boo-un râirk òrk gèe mohng?
รถไฟไป ... ขบวนแรกออกกี่โมง

When is the last train to ...?
rót fai bpai ... ka-boo-un sòOt tái òrk gèe mohng?
รถไฟไป ... ขบวนสุดท้ายออกกี่โมง

What is the fare to …?
kâh doy-ee săhn bpai … tâo-rài?

ค่าโดยสารไป … เท่าไร

Do I have to change?
dtôrng bplèe-un rót fai réu bplào?

ต้องเปลี่ยนรถไฟหรือเปล่า

Does the train stop at …?
rót fai yòOt têe … réu bplào?

รถไฟหยุดที่ … หรือเปล่า

How long does it take to get to …?
bpai … sěe-a way-lah nahn tâo-rài?

ไป … เสียเวลานานเท่าไร

A single/return ticket to … please
kǒr dtǒo-a bpai/bpai glùp …

ขอตั๋วไป / ไปกลับ …

I'd like to reserve a seat
kǒr jorng têe nûng

ขอจองที่นั่ง

Is this the right train for …?
rót fai ka-boo-un née bpai … châi mái?

รถไฟขบวนนี้ไป … ใช่ไหม

Is this the right platform for the … train?
têe nêe bpen chahn chah-lah bpai … châi réu bplào?

ที่นี่เป็นชานชาลาไป … ใช่หรือเปล่า

Which platform for the … train?
chahn chah-lah bpai … yòo têe-nǎi?

ชานชาลาไป … อยู่ที่ไหน

Could you help me with my luggage please?
chôo-ay yók gra-bpăo hâi nòy dâi mái?

ช่วยยกกระเป๋าให้หน่อยได้ไหม

Is this seat free?
têe nûng née wâhng réu bplào?

ที่นั่งนี้ว่างหรือเปล่า

This seat is taken
têe nûng née mâi wâhng

ที่นั่งนี้ไม่ว่าง

May I open the window?
kŏr bpèrt nâh-dtàhng nòy dâi mái?

ขอเปิดหน้าต่างหน่อยได้ไหม

May I close the window?
kŏr bpìt nâh-dtàhng nòy dâi mái?

ขอปิดหน้าต่างหน่อยได้ไหม

When do we arrive in ...?
tĕung ... gèe mohng?

ถึง ... กี่โมง

What station is this?
têe nêe sa-tăhn-nee a-rai?

ที่นี่สถานีอะไร

Do we stop at ...?
yòot têe ... réu bplào?

หยุดที่ ... หรือเปล่า

Would you keep an eye on my things for a moment?
chôo-ay fâo doo kŏrng hâi súk krôo dâi mái?

ช่วยเฝ้าดูของให้สักครู่ได้ไหม

THINGS YOU'LL SEE

ถึง	tĕung	arrivals
ออก	òrk	departures
ทางเข้า	tahng kâo	entrance
ทางออก	tahng òrk	exit
เต็ม	dtem	full
สอบถาม	sòrp tăhm	information
ที่ฝากกระเป๋า	têe fàhk gra-bpăo	left luggage
ห้ามเข้า	hâhm kâo	no entry
ห้ามสูบบุหรี่	hâhm sòop bOO-rèe	no smoking
ชานชาลา	chahn chah-lah	platform
ประชาสัมพันธ์	bpra-chah-sŭm-pun	public relations
จองแล้ว	jorng láir-o	reserved
รถนอน	rót norn	sleeping car
รถไฟไทย	rót fai tai	Thai State Railways
ที่จำหน่ายตั๋ว	têe jum-nài dtŏo-a	ticket office
ตารางเวลา	dtah-rahng way-lah	timetable
ว่าง	wâhng	vacant
ห้องพัก	hôrng púk	waiting room

THINGS YOU'LL HEAR

bpròht sâhp
Attention

kŏr doo dtŏo-a nòy krúp
Tickets please

41

BY BUS AND TAXI

For travelling around Bangkok there is a choice of ordinary bus, air-conditioned bus, samlor or tuk-tuk (the 3-wheeler motorized pedicab), or taxi. There is a fixed fare on ordinary buses, but on air-conditioned buses the fare depends on the distance covered. Street-maps indicating bus routes are available from book-stores and hotels. If you plan to go by samlor or taxi, check that the driver knows where you want to go and then agree the fare before stepping into the vehicle; it is normal to haggle a little over the price, but this should always be done with good humour. Tipping is not necessary. In provincial towns there may be some variations in the modes of public transport; there may be pedal-powered or motorcycle-powered samlors, or various-sized pick-up trucks operating a bus-cum-taxi service.

For travelling from Bangkok to various provinces the state-owned Mass Transport Organisation operates a cheap, frequent and efficient 'air-bus' (air-conditioned bus) from three major terminals in Bangkok; refreshments are usually served en route and on longer journeys a simple meal is provided at a regular stopping point. Private companies operate similar 'tour bus' services on various routes at very similar prices. Whether you travel by government or private-sector bus, it is nearly always necessary to book in advance – at the relevant terminus, in the case of the former, and from a central Bangkok office in the case of the latter.

USEFUL WORDS AND PHRASES

adult	pôo yài	ผู้ใหญ่
air-conditioned bus	rót air	รถแอร์
boat	reu-a	เรือ
bus	rót may	รถเมล์
bus stop	bpâi rót may	ป้ายรถเมล์

child	dèk	เด็ก
driver	kon kùp rót	คนขับรถ
fare	kâh doy-ee săhn	ค่าโดยสาร
ferry	reu-a kâhm fâhk	เรือข้ามฟาก
number 5 bus	rót may săi hâh	รถเมล์สาย ๕
passenger	pôo doy-ee săhn	ผู้โดยสาร
quay	tâh reu-a	ท่าเรือ
river	mâir náhm	แม่น้ำ
samlor	săhm-lór	สามล้อ
seat	têe nûng	ที่นั่ง
station	sa-tăhn-nee	สถานี
taxi	táirk-sêe	แท็กซี่
terminus	sa-tăhn-nee	สถานี
ticket	dtŏo-a	ตั๋ว
tour bus	rót too-a	รถทัวร์
traffic jam	rót dtìt	รถติด
'tuk tuk'	dtóok-dtóok	ตุ๊ก ๆ

Where is the bus station?
sa-tăhn-nee rót may yòo têe-năi?
สถานีรถเมล์อยู่ที่ไหน

Where is there a bus stop?
mee bpâi rót may yòo têe-năi?
มีป้ายรถเมล์อยู่ที่ไหน

Where do I get on the bus for ... ?
bpai ... kêun rót may têe-năi?
ไป ... ขึ้นรถเมล์ที่ไหน

What time does the bus for … leave?
rót bpai … òrk gèe mohng?

รถไป … ออกกี่โมง

Where do I book a ticket for …?
bpai … jorng dtŏo-a têe-năi?

ไป … จองตั๋วที่ไหน

Where do I buy a ticket for …?
bpai … séu dtŏo-a têe-năi?

ไป … ซื้อตั๋วที่ไหน

Which buses go to …?
bpai … ja kêun rót may săi năi?

ไป …จะขึ้นรถเมล์สายไหน

Would you tell me when we get to …?
tĕung … láir-o chôo-ay bòrk dôo-ay

ถึง … แล้วช่วยบอกด้วย

Do I have to get off yet?
dtôrng long dĕe-o née réu bplào?

ต้องลงเดี๋ยวนี้หรือเปล่า

How do you get to …?
bpai … bpai yung-ngai?

ไป … ไปอย่างไร

Is it very far?
glai mái?

ไกลไหม

I want to go to …
yàhk ja bpai …

อยากจะไป …

Do you go near …?
bpai tăir-o … réu bplào?

ไปแถว … หรือเปล่า

Could you close the window?
chôo-ay bpìt nâh-dtàhng nòy dâi mái?

ช่วยปิดหน้าต่างหน่อยได้ไหม

Could you open the window?
chôo-ay bpèrt nâh-dtàhng nòy dâi mái?

ช่วยเปิดหน้าต่างหน่อยได้ไหม

When does the last bus leave?
rót may têe-o sòOt tái òrk gèe mohng?

รถเมล์เที่ยวสุดท้ายออกกี่โมง

Do you know …?
róo-jùk … mái?

รู้จัก … ไหม

How much to go to …?
bpai … tâo-rài?

ไป … เท่าไร

That's a little expensive
pairng bpai nòy

แพงไปหน่อย

Will you go for … baht?
… bàht bpai mái?

… บาทไปไหม

Let's settle for … baht
… bàht gôr láir-o gun

… บาทก็แล้วกัน

Turn left/Turn right
lée-o sái/lée-o kwăh
เลี้ยวซ้าย / เลี้ยวขวา

Go straight on
ler-ee bpai èek
เลยไปอีก

Park over there/right here
jòrt têe-nôhn/dtrong née
จอดที่โน่น / ตรงนี้

THINGS YOU'LL SEE

รถปรับอากาศ	rót bprùp ah-gàht	air-conditioned bus
ถึง	tĕung	arrives
ออก	òrk	departs
สอบถาม	sòrp tăhm	enquiries
รับฝากของ	rúp fàhk kŏrng	left luggage
รถธรรมดา	rót tum-ma-dah	ordinary bus
ประชาสัมพันธ์	bpra-chah-sŭm-pun	public relations
ที่จำหน่ายตั๋ว	têe jum-nài dtŏo-a	ticket office
กำหนดเวลาเดินรถ	gum-nòt way-lah dern rót	timetable
สุขา หญิง - ชาย	sòo-kăh yĭng-chai	toilets (ladies-men)
รถทัวร์	rót too-a	tour bus
ห้องพักผู้โดยสาร	hôrng púk pôo-doy-ee sǎhn	waiting room

RESTAURANTS

Eating out is extremely popular in Thailand with a wide range of restaurants to cater for nearly all income levels. A traditional Thai meal consists of plain boiled rice with a number of side dishes such as a curry, fried vegetables, fried meat or fish and so on, which are shared between the diners; some such dishes are extremely hot to the western palate and it is perfectly reasonable to say, when making your order, **'mâi ao pèt mâhk na'** (not too hot, OK?). Thais use a spoon and fork rather than chopsticks, and a meal is a constant 'dipping in' process, taking a small portion from the side dish and eating it with the rice. If you are taken out for a meal, you may well be invited to select one of the side dishes; if you are worried about culinary faux-pas you can evade responsibility by saying, **'kOOn sùng hâi dee gwàh'** (it's better you order for me).

If you are eating alone or are in a hurry it is quicker to order individual dishes such as fried noodles, fried rice, noodle soup, duck-rice and so on from one of the ubiquitous Chinese noodle shops (where you will be offered chopsticks with your noodles). Pay for the meal at the end when you are ready to leave. If you have eaten in a cheap noodle shop, don't leave a tip; in more expensive premises, such as coffee shops, air-conditioned or open-air restaurants, a small tip is customary. If you are taken out for a meal, don't offer to pay your share of the bill; you will probably have a chance to reciprocate as host at a later date.

USEFUL WORDS AND PHRASES

ashtray	têe-kèe-a bOO-rèe	ที่เขี่ยบุหรี่
beer	bee-a	เบียร์
bill	bin	บิล
bottle	kòo-ut	ขวด
bowl	chahm	ชาม

cake	ka-nŏm káyk	ขนมเค้ก
chef	pôr kroo-a	พ่อครัว
chopsticks	dta-gèe-up	ตะเกียบ
cigarettes	bOO-rèe	บุหรี่
coffee	gah-fair	กาแฟ
cup	tôo-ay	ถ้วย
fish sauce	núm bplah	น้ำปลา
fork	sôrm	ส้อม
glass	gâir-o	แก้ว
knife	mêet	มีด
matches	mái kèet	ไม้ขีด
menu	may-noo	เมนู
milk	nom	นม
plate	jahn	จาน
receipt	bai sèt rúp ngern	ใบเสร็จรับเงิน
sandwich	sairn-wít	แซ็นวิช
serviette	pâh chét meu	ผ้าเช็ดมือ
snack	ah-hăhn wâhng	อาหารว่าง
soup	sóOp	ซุป
spoon	chórn	ช้อน
sugar	núm dtahn	น้ำตาล
table	dtó	โต๊ะ
tea	núm chah	น้ำชา
teaspoon	chórn chah	ช้อนชา
tip	ngern típ	เงินทิป
waiter	kon sèrp	คนเสริฟ
waitress	kon sèrp yĭng	คนเสริฟหญิง
water	náhm	น้ำ

A table for one please
kŏr dtó sŭm-rùp kon dee-o

ขอโต๊ะสำหรับคนเดียว

A table for two please
kŏr dtó sŭm-rùp sŏrng kon

ขอโต๊ะสำหรับสองคน

Can I see the menu?
kŏr doo may-noo nòy

ขอดูเมนูหน่อย

What would you recommend?
kOOn ja náir-num a-rai?

คุณจะแนะนำอะไร

It's better you order for me
kOOn sùng hâi dee gwàh

คุณสั่งให้ดีกว่า

Do you have ...?
mee ... mái?

มี ... ไหม

I'd like ...
kŏr ...

ขอ ...

Not too hot, O.K.?
mâi ao pèt mâhk ná

ไม่เอาเผ็ดมากนะ

Is it (very) hot?
pèt mâhk mái?

เผ็ดมากไหม

I can't eat hot food
tahn ah-hǎhn pèt mâi bpen

ทานอาหารเผ็ดไม่เป็น

I can eat Thai food
tahn ah-hǎhn tai bpen

ทานอาหารไทยเป็น

Could I have a glass of water please?
kǒr núm kǎirng bplào gâir-o nèung

ขอน้ำแข็งเปล่าแก้วหนึ่ง

Just a cup of coffee, please
kǒr gah-fair tôo-ay nèung tâo-nún

ขอกาแฟถ้วยหนึ่งเท่านั้น

Waiter/waitress!
kOOn krúp (ká)!

คุณครับ (คะ)

Can we have the bill, please?
kǒr bin nòy krúp (kâ)

ขอบิลหน่อยครับ (ค่ะ)

I didn't order this
nêe mâi dâi sùng krúp (kâ)

นี่ไม่ได้สั่งครับ (ค่ะ)

May we have some more ...?
kǒr ... èek nòy dâi mái?

ขอ ... อีกหน่อยได้ไหม

That was an excellent meal, thank you
a-ròy mâhk krúp (kâ)

อร่อยมากครับ (ค่ะ)

YOU MAY HEAR

sùng láir-o réu yung krúp (ká)?
Have you ordered yet?
*(answer: **yung** = no; **sùng láir-o** = yes)*

a-ròy mái krúp (ká)?
Are you enjoying your meal, sir/madam?
*(answer: **a-ròy** = yes; **mâi a-ròy** = no)*

sùng a-rai èek mái?
Do you want to order anything else?

THINGS YOU'LL SEE

| ร้านอาหาร | ráhn ah-hăhn | restaurant |
| ภัตตาคาร | pút-dtah-kahn | restaurant |

STARTERS

ขนมจีบ	**ka-nǒm jèep**	'dim sum', pieces of meat in dough
ทอดมัน	**tôrt mun**	fish-cakes
สะเต๊ะ หมู ไก่	**sa-dtáy mǒo, gài**	'satay', pork, chicken
กุ้งเผา	**gôong pǎo**	shrimps grilled over charcoal
ปอเปี๊ยะทอด	**bpor bpêe-a tôrt**	spring roll
อาหารว่าง	**ah-hǎhn wâhng**	starters

SOUPS AND CURRIES

แกงเนื้อ	**gairng néu-a**	beef curry
แกงเขียวหวาน	**gairng kěe-o wǎhn**	beef curry in a green sauce
แกงไก่	**gairng gài**	chicken curry
ต้มยำไก่	**dtôm yum gài**	chicken 'tom yam'
พะแนง	**pa-nairng**	'dry' curry
แกงกะหรี่	**gairng ga-rèe**	Indian-style curry
แกงมัสหมั่น	**gairng mút-sa-mùn**	'Muslim' curry
ต้มยำกุ้ง	**dtôm yum gôong**	shrimp 'tom yam'
แกงส้ม	**gairng sôm**	vegetable curry (spicy)
แกงจืด	**gairng jèut**	vegetable soup or stock (bland)
ต้มยำ	**dtôm yum**	'tom yam', a spicy dish
แกง	**gairng**	'wet' curry
แกงเผ็ด	**gairng pèt**	spicy curry

EGG DISHES

ไข่ลวก	**kài lôo-uk**	boiled egg (served in a glass, very soft, almost raw)
ไข่	**kài**	egg
ไข่พะโล้	**kài pa-lóh**	egg stewed in soy sauce
ไข่ดาว	**kài dao**	fried egg
ไข่เจียว	**kài jee-o**	omelette (deep-fried)
ไข่ยัดไส้	**kài yút sâi**	omelette (stuffed)
ไข่ลูกเขย	**kài lôok kěr-ee**	'son-in-law' eggs (hard-boiled with various condiments)

SEAFOOD

ปู	**bpoo**	crab
ปลา	**bplah**	fish
กุ้งทอดกระเทียมพริกไทย	**gôong tôrt gra-tee-um prík tai**	prawns fried with garlic and pepper
กุ้ง	**gôong**	shrimps, prawns
กุ้งผัดพริก	**gôong pùt prík**	shrimps fried with chillies
กุ้งผัดใบกระเพรา	**gôong pùt bai gra-prao**	shrimps fried with basil leaves
ปลาหมึก	**bplah-mèuk**	squid
ปลาหมึกผัดพริก	**bplah-mèuk pùt prík**	squid fried with chillies

ปลาหมึกทอด กระเทียมพริกไทย	**bplah-mèuk tôrt gra-tee-um prík tai**	squid fried with garlic and pepper
ปลาเปรี้ยวหวาน	**bplah bprêe-o wǎhn**	sweet and sour fish

MEAT DISHES
Beef

เนื้อ	**néu-a**	beef
เนื้อผัดน้ำมันหอย	**néu-a pùt núm mun hǒy**	beef fried in oyster sauce
เนื้อสับผัดพริก กระเพรา	**néu-a sùp pùt prík gra-prao**	beef minced and fried with chillies and basil
เนื้อผัดกระเทียม พริกไทย	**néu-a pùt gra-tee-um prík tai**	beef fried with garlic and pepper
เนื้อผัดขิง	**néu-a pùt kǐng**	beef fried with ginger

Chicken

ไก่	**gài**	chicken
ไก่ผัดหน่อไม้	**gài pùt nòr-mái**	chicken fried with bamboo shoots
ไก่ผัดใบกระเพรา	**gài pùt bai gra-prao**	chicken fried with basil leaves
ไก่ผัดเม็ดมะม่วง หิมพานต์	**gài pùt mét ma-môo-ung hǐm-ma-pahn**	chicken fried with cashew nuts
ไก่ผัดพริก	**gài pùt prík**	chicken fried with chillies

ไก่ทอดกระเทียม	**gài tôrt gra-tee-**	chicken fried with
พริกไทย	**um prík tai**	garlic and pepper
ไก่ผัดขิง	**gài pùt kǐng**	chicken fried with
		ginger
ไก่ย่าง	**gài yâhng**	chicken served
		roasted or
		barbecued

Duck

| เป็ด | **bpèt** | duck |
| เป็ดย่าง | **bpèt yâhng** | roast duck |

Pork

หมู	**mǒo**	pork
หมูสับผัดพริกกระเพรา	**mǒo sùp pùt**	pork minced and
	prík gra-prao	fried with chillies
		and basil
หมูผัดพริก	**mǒo pùt prík**	pork fried with
		chillies
หมูทอดกระเทียม	**mǒo tǒrt gra-tee-**	pork fried with
พริกไทย	**um prík tai**	garlic and pepper
หมูผัดขิง	**mǒo pùt kǐng**	pork fried with ginger
หมูเปรี้ยวหวาน	**mǒo bprêe-o**	sweet and sour pork
	wǎhn	

RICE AND RICE DISHES

ข้าวสวย	**kâo sǒo-ay**	boiled rice
ข้าวผัดไก่	**kâo pùt gài**	chicken fried rice
ข้าวมันไก่	**kâo mun gài**	chicken rice
ข้าวผัดปู	**kâo pùt bpoo**	crab fried rice

ข้าวหน้าเป็ด	**kâo nâh bpèt**	duck rice
ข้าวผัด	**kâo pùt**	fried rice
ข้าวผัดหมู	**kâo pùt mǒo**	pork fried rice
ข้าวหมูแดง	**kâo mǒo dairng**	'red' pork rice
ข้าว	**kâo**	rice
ข้าวคลุกกะปิ	**kâo klóok ga-bpì**	rice fried with shrimp paste and served with sweet pork and shredded omelette
ข้าวต้ม	**kâo dtôm**	rice 'porridge'
ข้าวผัดกุ้ง	**kâo pùt gôong**	shrimp fried rice
ข้าวเหนียว	**kâo něe-o**	'sticky' rice

NOODLES AND NOODLE DISHES

หมี่กรอบ	**mèe gròrp**	crispy noodles
ก๋วยเตี๋ยวแห้ง	**gǒo-ay dtěe-o hâirng**	'dry' noodles (without soup)
บะหมี่	**ba-mèe**	egg noodles
ผัดซีอิ๊ว	**pùt see éw**	noodles fried in soy sauce
ผัดราดหน้า	**pùt râht nâh**	noodles served with fried meat and vegetables in a thick gravy
ก๋วยเตี๋ยวน้ำ	**gǒo-ay dtěe-o náhm**	noodle soup
ก๋วยเตี๋ยว	**gǒo-ay dtěe-o**	rice-flour noodles

| ผัดไทย | **pùt tai** | Thai-style fried noodles |
| ขนมจีน | **ka-nǒm jeen** | Thai vermicelli |

VEGETABLES

หน่อไม้	**nòr mái**	bamboo shoots
ถั่วงอก	**tòo-a ngôrk**	bean sprouts
กระหล่ำปลี	**gra-lùm-bplee**	cabbage
พริก	**prík**	chilli
ถั่วฝักยาว	**tòo-a fùk yao**	cowpea
แตงกวา	**dtairng-gwah**	cucumber
กระเทียม	**gra-tee-um**	garlic
ขิง	**king**	ginger
พริกหยวก	**prík yòo-uk**	green pepper
ถั่วลันเตา	**tòo-a lun-dtao**	mange-tout
ผักบุ้ง	**pùk bôong**	morning glory
เห็ด	**hèt**	mushroom
หัวหอม	**hǒo-a hǒrm**	onion
ผักคะน้า	**pùk ka-náh**	spring greens
ต้นหอม	**dtôn hǒrm**	spring onion
ข้าวโพด	**kâo pôht**	sweet corn
มะเขือเทศ	**ma-kěu-a tâyt**	tomato
ผัก	**pùk**	vegetable

FRUIT

กล้วย	**glôo-ay**	banana
มะพร้าว	**ma-práo**	coconut
น้อยหน่า	**nóy-nàh**	custard apple

ทุเรียน	**tOO-ree-un**	durian
ผลไม้	**pǒn-la-mái**	fruit
ฝรั่ง	**fa-rùng**	guava
ขนุน	**ka-nǒon**	jackfruit
ลำใย	**lum-yai**	longan
ลิ้นจี่	**lín-jèe**	lychee
มะม่วง	**ma-môo-ung**	mango
ส้ม	**sôm**	orange
มะละกอ	**ma-la-gor**	papaya
สับปะรด	**sùp-bpa-rót**	pineapple
ส้มโอ	**sôm oh**	pomelo
เงาะ	**ngór**	rambutan
ชมพู่	**chom-pôo**	rose apple
ละมุด	**la-móot**	sapodilla
แตงโม	**dtairng moh**	water melon

BASIC CONDIMENTS AND METHODS OF COOKING

ต้ม	**dtôm**	boiled
ย่าง	**yâhng**	charcoal-grilled
น้ำพริก	**núm prík**	chilli paste
น้ำปลา	**núm bplah**	fish sauce
ทอด	**tôrt**	fried, deep-fried
ผัด	**pùt**	fried, stir-fried
อบ	**òp**	oven-cooked
พริกไทย	**prík tai**	pepper
น้ำซีอิ๊ว	**núm see éw**	soy sauce
ปิ้ง	**bpîng**	toasted
น้ำส้ม	**núm sôm**	vinegar

DRINKS

เบียร์	**bee-a**	beer
โคล่า	**koh-lâh**	Coca Cola ®
น้ำมะพร้าว	**núm ma-práo**	coconut juice
กาแฟ	**gah-fair**	coffee
โอเลี้ยง	**oh-lée-ung**	coffee served black, iced and with lots of sugar
เครื่องดื่ม	**krêu-ung dèum**	drink(s)
น้ำผลไม้	**núm pǒn-la-mái**	fruit juice
น้ำแข็ง	**núm kǎirng**	ice
น้ำมะนาว	**núm ma-nao**	lime juice
แม่โขง	**mâir-kǒhng**	Mekhong Whisky ®
น้ำส้ม	**núm sôm**	orange juice (bottled)
น้ำส้มคั้น	**núm sôm kún**	orange juice (fresh)
เป๊ปซี่	**bpép-sêe**	Pepsi Cola ®
น้ำโปลาริส	**núm bpoh-la-rít**	Polaris water ® (bottled drinking water)
น้ำโซดา	**núm soh-dah**	soda water
น้ำชา	**núm chah**	tea
น้ำ	**náhm**	water
น้ำแข็งเปล่า	**núm kǎirng bplào**	water, a glass of water with ice

SHOPPING

Thailand offers the visitor a wide variety of shopping facilities ranging from traditional markets to ultra-modern multi-storeyed shopping plazas. Shops vary in their opening times, but many stay open until 7 or 8 p.m. during the week and remain open on Sundays. While bargaining is inappropriate in most shops, it is an essential part of shopping in markets and at pavement stalls; ideally, you should try to get some idea of what a reasonable price is before attempting to haggle and then negotiations should be carried out in a good-humoured manner.

USEFUL WORDS AND PHRASES

bookshop	ráhn kăi núng-sĕu	ร้านขายหนังสือ
to buy	séu	ซื้อ
cheap	tòok	ถูก
chemist	ráhn kăi yah	ร้านขายยา
department store	hâhng	ห้าง
fashion	fair-chûn	แฟชั่น
gold	torng	ทอง
hill-tribe handicrafts hùt-ta-gum chao kăo		หัตถกรรมชาวเขา
ladies' wear	séu-pâh sa-dtree	เสื้อผ้าสตรี
market	dta-làht	ตลาด
menswear	séu-pâh boo-ròot	เสื้อผ้าบุรุษ
newsagent	ráhn kăi núng-sĕu pim	ร้านขายหนังสือพิมพ์
price	rah-kah	ราคา
receipt	bai sèt rúp ngern	ใบเสร็จรับเงิน

sale	lót rah-kah	ลดราคา
shoe shop	ráhn kǎi rorng táo	ร้านขายรองเท้า
shop	ráhn	ร้าน
to go shopping	bpai séu kǒrng	ไปซื้อของ
silverware	krêu-ung ngern	เครื่องเงิน
special offer	lót pi-sàyt	ลดพิเศษ
to spend	sěe-a ngern	เสียเงิน
stationer	ráhn kǎi krêu-ung kěe-un	ร้านขายเครื่องเขียน
supermarket	sóop-bpêr-mah-gêt	ซุปเปอร์มาร์เก็ต
tailor	ráhn dtùt sêu-a	ร้านตัดเสื้อ
Thai silk	pâh-mǎi tai	ผ้าไหมไทย
till	têe chum-rá ngern	ที่ชำระเงิน
travel agent	bor-ri-sùt num têe-o	บริษัทนำเที่ยว

I'd like ...
dtôrng-gahn ...
ต้องการ ...

Do you have ...?
mee ... mái?
มี ... ไหม

How much is this?
nêe tâo-rài?
นี่เท่าไร

Where is the ... department?
pa-nàirk kǎi ... yòo têe-nǎi?
แผนกขาย ... อยู่ที่ไหน

Do you have any more of these?
yàhng née mee èek mái?
อย่างนี้มีอีกไหม

I'd like to change this please
kŏr bplèe-un un née nòy dâi mái?
ขอเปลี่ยนอันนี้หน่อยได้ไหม

Have you anything cheaper?
tòok gwàh née mee mái?
ถูกกว่านี้มีไหม

Have you anything larger?
yài gwàh née mee mái?
ใหญ่กว่านี้มีไหม

Have you anything smaller?
lék gwàh née mee mái?
เล็กกว่านี้มีไหม

Does it come in other colours?
mee sĕe èun èek mái?
มีสีอื่นอีกไหม

Could you wrap it for me?
chôo-ay hòr hâi nòy dâi mái?
ช่วยห่อให้หน่อยได้ไหม

Can I have a receipt?
kŏr bai sèt rúp ngern
ขอใบเสร็จรับเงิน

Can I try it (them) on?
kŏr lorng sài doo dâi mái?
ขอลองใส่ดูได้ไหม

Where do I pay?
jài ngern têe-năi?
จ่ายเงินที่ไหน

Can I have a refund?
kŏr keun ngern hâi dâi mái?
ขอคืนเงินให้ได้ไหม

I'm just looking
chom doo tâo-nún
ชมดูเท่านั้น

I'll come back later
dĕe-o ja glùp mah mài
เดี๋ยวจะกลับมาใหม่

That's a bit expensive
pairng bpai nòy krúp (kâ)
แพงไปหน่อยครับ (ค่ะ)

Could you lower the price a little?
lót rah-kah nòy dâi mái?
ลดราคาหน่อยได้ไหม

How about ... baht?
...bàht dâi mái?
...บาทได้ไหม

THINGS YOU'LL SEE

บาท	bàht	baht
ปิด	bpìt	closed
ใบละ ...	bai la ...	... each
ชั้น	chún	floor →

63

เปิด	bpèrt	open
โหลละ ...	lŏh la ...	... per dozen
กิโลละ ...	gi-loh la ...	... per kilogram
ราคา	rah-kah	price
ลดราคา	lót rah-kah	sale
ลดพิเศษ	lót pi-sàyt	special reduction

THINGS YOU'LL HEAR

rúp a-rai krúp (ká)?
Are you being served?

mee sàyt sa-dtahng mái krúp (ká)?
Have you any smaller money?

dtorn née kǎi mòt krúp (kâ)
I'm sorry we're out of stock

mee tâo née la krúp (kâ)
This is all we have

séu a-rai èek mái krúp (ká)?
Will there be anything else?

AT THE HAIRDRESSER

Appearance is very important in Thailand and hairdressers and barbers catering to a wide variety of income levels are plentiful. The most sophisticated salons in Bangkok are similar to those in the west; even more modest premises usually offer a full range of beauty care and often double as dressmakers too. It is generally not necessary to make an appointment.

USEFUL WORDS AND PHRASES

appointment	nút	นัด
beard	krao	เครา
blond	pŏm sĕe torng	ผมสีทอง
blow dry	bpào hâi hâirng	เป่าให้แห้ง
brush	bprairng pŏm	แปรงผม
comb	wĕe	หวี
conditioner	kreem nôo-ut pŏm	ครีมนวดผม
curlers	krêu-ung dùt pŏm	เครื่องดัดผม
curling tongs	keem dùt pŏm	คีมดัดผม
curly	pŏm yìk	ผมหยิก
dark	dum	ดำ
fringe	pŏm máh	ผมม้า
gel	kreem sài pŏm	ครีมใส่ผม
hair	pŏm	ผม
haircut	dtùt pŏm	ตัดผม
hairdresser		
(person)	chûng dtùt pŏm	ช่างตัดผม
(shop)	ráhn dtùt pŏm	ร้านตัดผม

AT THE HAIRDRESSER

hairdryer	krêu-ung bpào pǒm	เครื่องเป่าผม
long	yao	ยาว
moustache	nòo-ut	หนวด
parting	sàirk	แสก
perm	dùt pǒm	ดัดผม
shampoo	yah sà pom	ยาสระผม
shave	gohn	โกน
shaving foam	kreem gohn nòo-ut	ครีมโกนหนวด
short	sûn	สั้น
styling mousse	kreem dtàirng pǒm	ครีมแต่งผม
wash and set	sà sét	สระเซ็ท
wavy	bpen lorn	เป็นลอน

I'd like to make an appointment
yàhk nút way-lah tum pǒm
อยากนัดเวลาทำผม

Just a trim please
dtùt nít-nòy tâo-nún
ตัดนิดหน่อยเท่านั้น

Not too much off
mâi dtùt òrk mâhk
ไม่ตัดออกมาก

A bit more off here please
dtùt dtrong née òrk èek nòy
ตัดตรงนี้ออกอีกหน่อย

I'd like a cut and blow-dry
yàhk ja dtùt láir bpào hâi hâirng
อยากจะตัดและเป่าให้แห้ง

THINGS YOU'LL SEE

บาร์เบอร์	bah-ber	barber
เสริมสวย	sěrm sǒo-ay	beauty care
ตัดเสื้อ	dtùt sêu-a	dressmaker's
แต่งหน้า	dtàirng nâh	facial
นวดหน้า	nôo-ut nâh	facial massage
ตัดผม	dtùt pǒm	hair cut
ดัดผม	dùt pǒm	hair styling
ทำเล็บ	tum lép	manicure
เซ็ทผม	sét pǒm	set
โกนหนวด	gohn nòo-ut	shave
สระ	sà	wash

THINGS YOU'LL HEAR

yàhk ja tum bàirp nǎi?
How would you like it?

kâir née sûn por réu yung?
Is that short enough?

ja sài kreem nôo-ut pǒm mái?
Would you like any conditioner?

POST OFFICES AND BANKS

Thailand has an extremely efficient postal system. Generally, post offices are open 8.30-4.30 on weekdays but remain closed at weekends. Bangkok's Central Post Office on New Road, however, opens on Saturday and Sunday mornings also and, in addition to normal post office services, offers a parcel-packing service and 24 hour telegram service. Stamps can also be purchased from and letters posted at major hotels.

Banks open from 8.30-3.30 on weekdays. Many banks in Bangkok also operate currency exchange kiosks outside the main building and these often remain open until 8 p.m., seven days a week. Currency exchange facilities are also available at Bangkok's Don Muang airport (24 hour service) and at major hotels but the latter are generally less favourable.

Currency: 1 baht = 100 satang

USEFUL WORDS AND PHRASES

aerogramme	jòt-mǎi ah-gàht	จดหมายอากาศ
airmail	tahng ah-gàht	ทางอากาศ
baht *(currency)*	bàht	บาท
bank	ta-nah-kahn	ธนาคาร
banknote	ta-nah-bùt/báirnk	ธนาบัตร; แบ็งค์
to change	lâirk bplèe-un	แลกเปลี่ยน
cheque	chék	เช็ค
collection	gèp jòt-mǎi jàhk dtôo	เก็บจดหมายจากตู้
counter	káo-dtêr	เคาน์เตอร์
customs form	form sěe-a pah-sěe	ฟอร์มเสียภาษี
delivery	sòng jòt-mǎi dtahm bâhn	ส่งจดหมายตามบ้าน

to deposit	fàhk ngern	ฝากเงิน
exchange rate	ùt-dtrah lâirk bplèe-un	อัตราแลกเปลี่ยน
form	bàirp form	แบบเฟอร์ม
letter	jòt-mǎi	จดหมาย
letter box	dtôo bprai-sa-nee	ตู้ไปรษณีย์
mail *(noun)*	jòt-mǎi	จดหมาย
money order	ta-nah-nút	ธนาณัติ
package/parcel	hòr	ห่อ
to post	sòng jòt-mǎi	ส่งจดหมาย
postage rates	ùt-dtrah kâh bprai-sa-nee	อัตราค่าไปรษณีย์
postal order	ta-nah-nút	ธนาณัติ
postcard	póht-gáht	โปสการ์ด
postcode	ra-hùt bprai-sa-nee	รหัสไปรษณีย์
poste-restante	poste restante	poste restante
postman	bOO-ròot bprai-sa-nee	บุรุษไปรษณีย์
post office	bprai-sa-nee	ไปรษณีย์
pound sterling	ngern bporn sa-dter-ling	เงินปอนด์สเตอร์ลิง
registered letter	jòt-mǎi long ta-bee-un	จดหมายลงทะเบียน
satang *(currency)*	sa-dtahng	สตางค์
stamp	sa-dtairm	แสตมป์
surface mail	sòng tahng reu-a	ส่งทางเรือ
telegram	toh-ra-lâyk	โทรเลข
traveller's cheque	chék dern tahng	เช็คเดินทาง

How much is a letter/postcard to …?
sòng jòt-mǎi/póht-gáht bpai … tâo-rài?

ส่งจดหมาย /โปสการ์ดไป … เท่าไร

I would like three 9 baht stamps
kǒr sa-dtairm bpèe gâo bàht sǎhm doo-ung

ขอแสตมป์เก้าบาทสามดวง

I want to register this letter
jòt-mǎi née yàhk ja long ta-bee-un

จดหมายนี้อยากจะลงทะเบียน

I want to send this parcel to …
hòr née yàhk ja sòng bpai …

ห่อนี้อยากจะส่งไป …

How long does the post to … take?
sòng bpai … chái way-lah nahn tâo-rài?

ส่งไป … ใช้เวลานานเท่าไร

Where can I post this?
nêe sòng dâi têe-nǎi?

นี้ส่งได้ที่ไหน

Is there any mail for me?
mee jòt-mǎi sǔm-rùp pǒm (dee-chún) mái?

มีจดหมายสำหรับผม (ดิฉัน) ไหม

I'd like to send a telegram to …
dtôrng-gahn sòng toh-ra-lâyk bpai …

ต้องการส่งโทรเลขไป …

This is to go airmail
nêe sòng bpai tahng ah-gàht

นี้ส่งไปทางอากาศ

I'd like to change this into ...
kǒr lâirk nêe bpen ...

ขอแลกนี่เป็น ...

Can I cash these traveller's cheques?
kǒr lâirk chék dern tahng dâi mái?

ขอแลกเช็คเดินทางได้ไหม

What is the exchange rate for the pound?
ùt-dtrah lâirk bplèe-un ngern bporn tâo-rài?

อัตราแลกเปลี่ยนเงินปอนด์เท่าไร

THINGS YOU'LL SEE

ที่อยู่	têe yòo	address
ทางอากาศ	tahng ah-gàht	airmail
กรุงเทพ ฯ	grOOng-tâyp	Bangkok
ธนาคาร	ta-nah-kahn	bank
ฝากเงิน	fàhk ngern	deposits
สอบถาม	sòrp tǎhm	enquiries
อัตราแลกเปลี่ยน	ùt-dtrah lâirk	exchange rate
เงินตราต่างประเทศ	bplèe-un ngern	
	dtrah dtàhng	
	bpra-tâyt	
ด่วน	dòo-un	express
กรอก	gròrk	to fill in
แลกเปลี่ยนเงินตรา	lâirk bplèe-un	foreign exchange
ต่างประเทศ	ngern dtrah	
	dtàhng bpra-tâyt	→

71

ตู้ไปรษณีย์	dtôo bprai-sa-nee	letterbox
จดหมาย	jòt-mǎi	letters
เวลาปิด-เปิด	way-lah bpìt – bpèrt	opening hours
ที่อื่น	têe èun	other places
พัสดุ	pú-sa-dòo	parcels (counter)
ไปรษณีย์	bprai-sa-nee	post office
ที่ทำการไปรษณีย์	têe tum gahn bprai-sa-nee	post office
ลงทะเบียน	long ta-bee-un	registered mail
ผู้ส่ง	pôo sòng	sender
ไปรษณียกร	bprai-sa-nee-ya-gorn	stamps
โทรเลข	toh-rah-lâyk	telegrams
ถอนเงิน	tǒrn ngern	withdrawals

THINGS YOU'LL HEAR

gròrk bàirp form née
Fill in this form

kǒr doo núng-sěu dern tahng nòy dâi mái?
Could I see your passport please?

sòng bpai tahng ah-gàht réu tahng reu-a?
Do you want to send it by air or surface mail?

TELEPHONING

Telephone calls can be made from public kiosks, hotels and some shops. Baht coins come in three different sizes and only the smaller size will fit in the standard pay-phone. While direct dialling is possible, it is often easier for long-distance calls to enlist the aid of the operator at a large hotel; alternatively, when in Bangkok, such calls can be made from an annex to the Central General Post Office just off New Road.

USEFUL WORDS AND PHRASES

to call toh-ra-sùp   โทรศัพท์
code ra-hùt toh-ra-sùp   รหัสโทรศัพท์
to dial mǒon ber   หมุนเบอร์
extension dtòr   ต่อ
international call toh-ra-sùp   โทรศัพท์ต่างประเทศ
  dtàhng bpra-tâyt
number ber toh-ra-sùp   เบอร์โทรศัพท์
operator pa-núk ngahn toh-ra sùp   พนักงานโทรศัพท์
receiver hǒo toh-ra-sùp   หูโทรศัพท์
reverse charge call toh-ra-sùp   โทรศัพท์เก็บเงินปลายทาง
  gèp ngern bplai tahng
telephone toh-ra-sùp   โทรศัพท์
telephone box dtôo toh-ra-sùp   ตู้โทรศัพท์
telephone directory sa-mòot   สมุดหมายเลข
  mǎi-lâyk toh-ra-sùp   โทรศัพท์
wrong number toh pìt   โทรผิด

Where is the nearest phone box?
tăir-o née mee dtôo toh-ra-sùp yòo têe-năi?

แถวนี้มีตู้โทรศัพท์อยู่ที่ไหน

Is there a telephone directory?
mee sa-mòot măi-lâyk toh-ra-sùp mái?

มีสมุดหมายเลขโทรศัพท์ไหม

Can I call abroad from here?
ja toh-ra-sùp bpai dtàhng bpra-tâyt jàhk têe nee dâi mái?

จะโทรศัพท์ไปต่างประเทศจากที่นี่ได้ไหม

How much is a call to ...?
toh-ra-sùp bpai ... tâo-rài?

โทรศัพท์ไป ... เท่าไร

I would like to reverse the charges
kŏr hâi gèp ngern bplai tahng

ขอให้เก็บเงินปลายทาง

I would like a number in ...
dtôrng-gahn dtòr ber toh-ra-sùp têe ...

ต้องการต่อเบอร์โทรศัพท์ที่ ...

Hello, this is ... speaking
hello, pŏm (dee-chún) ... pôot krúp (kâ)

ฮัลโหล ผม (ดิฉัน) ... พูดครับ (คะ)

Is that ...?
têe-nôhn ... châi mái?

ที่โน่น ... ใช่ไหม

Speaking
gum-lung pôot krúp (kâ)

กำลังพูดครับ (ค่ะ)

I would like to speak to ...
kŏr pôot gùp ... nòy, dâi mái?

ขอพูดกับ ... หน่อยได้ไหม

Extension ... please
kŏr dtòr ber ...

ขอต่อเบอร์ ...

Please tell him ... called
chôo-ay bòrk káo wâh mee ... toh mah

ช่วยบอกเขาว่ามี ... โทรมา

Could you ask him to call me back please?
chôo-ay hâi káo toh mah mài

ช่วยให้เขาโทรมาใหม่

My number is ...
ber toh-ra-sùp pŏm (dee-chún) ...

เบอร์โทรศัพท์ผม (ดิฉัน) ...

Do you know where he is?
sâhp mái wâh káo yòo têe-năi?

ทราบไหมว่าเขาอยู่ที่ไหน

When will he be back?
káo ja glùp mah mêu-rai?

เขาจะกลับมาเมื่อไร

Could I leave him a message?
kŏr fàhk sùng a-rai nòy dâi mái?

ขอฝากสั่งอะไรหน่อยได้ไหม

I'll ring back later
dĕe-o ja toh mah mài

เดี๋ยวจะโทรมาใหม่

Sorry, wrong number
kŏr-tôht toh pìt ber

ขอโทษไทรผิดเบอร์

THINGS YOU'LL SEE

บาท	bàht	baht *(unit of currency)*
รหัส	ra-hùt	code
เหรียญ	rĕe-un	coin
ต่อ	dtòr	extension
ต่างประเทศ	dtàhng bpra-tâyt	international
โทรศัพท์ต่างประเทศ	toh-ra-sùp dtàhng bpra-tâyt	international call(s)
โทรศัพท์ทางไกล	toh-ra-sùp tahng glai	long-distance call(s)
เสีย	sĕe-a	out of order
ตู้โทรศัพท์สาธารณะ	dtôo toh-ra-sùp săh-tah-ra-ná	public telephone box
โทรศัพท์	toh-ra-sùp	telephone

REPLIES YOU MAY BE GIVEN

ja pôot gùp krai krúp (ká)?
Who would you like to speak to?

koon toh ber pìt
You've got the wrong number

$\rightarrow$

krai pôot krúp (ká)?
Who's speaking?

ber toh-ra-sùp koon tâo-rài krúp (ká)?
What is your number?

pôot dung dung nòy dâi mái?
Could you speak louder please?

káo mâi yòo krúp (kâ)
Sorry, he's not in

káo ja glùp ... mohng
He'll be back at ... o'clock

chôo-ay toh mah mài prôong-née krúp (ká)
Please call again tomorrow

ja bòrk káo wâh koon toh mah
I'll tell him you called

mee a-rai ja sùng mái?
Do you want to leave a message?

dtòr ber a-rai krúp (ká)?
What extension number do you want?

săi mâi wâhng
The line's engaged

HEALTH

In the event of serious injury or illness, medical expenses can prove costly, so medical insurance is essential. Appointments to see a doctor at a private hospital or clinic can be made at short notice. All doctors will be able to speak English and many will have spent a number of years of further training or practice in America. Thai doctors are sometimes rather liberal in the types and quantities of medicines they prescribe, even for relatively minor illnesses; if you are unhappy about the prescription discuss it with the doctor. For small problems, it is possible to seek advice and purchase the appropriate medicines from a chemist without a prescription.

USEFUL WORDS AND PHRASES

accident	OO-bùt-dti-hàyt	อุบัติเหตุ
acupuncture	fŭng kĕm	ฝังเข็ม
ambulance	rót pa-yah-bahn	รถพยาบาล
anaemic	loh-hìt jahng	โลหิตจาง
appendicitis	rôhk sâi dtìng	โรคไส้ติ่ง
appendix	sâi dtìng	ไส้ติ่ง
aspirin	air-sa-bprin	แอสไพริน
asthma	rôhk hèut	โรคหืด
backache	bpòo-ut lŭng	ปวดหลัง
bandage	pâh pun plăir	ผ้าพันแผล
bite *(by dog)*	măh gùt	หมากัด
(by insect)	ma-lairng gùt	แมลงกัด
bladder	gra-pór bpù-săh-wá	กระเพาะปัสสาวะ
blister	plăir porng	แผลพอง
blood	lêu-ut	เลือด

78

blood donor pôo bor-ri-jàhk lêu-ut   ผู้บริจาคเลือด

burn *(noun)* mâi   ไหม้

cancer ma-reng   มะเร็ง

chemist ráhn kăi yah   ร้านขายยา

chest nâh-òk   หน้าอก

chickenpox ee-sòok ee-săi   อีสุกอีใส

cholera a-hi-wah   อหิวาต์

cold *(noun)* bpen wùt   เป็นหวัด

concussion sa-mŏrng tòok gra-tóp gra-teu-un   สมองถูกกระทบ กระเทือน

constipation tórng pòok   ท้องผูก

contact lenses korn-táirk layn   คอนแทคท์เลนส์

corn dtah bplah   ตาปลา

cough *(noun)* ai   ไอ

cut *(noun)* roy bàht   รอยบาด

dentist mŏr fun   หมอฟัน

diabetes rôhk bao wăhn   โรคเบาหวาน

diarrhoea tórng sĕe-a   ท้องเสีย

dizzy wee-un hŏo-a   เวียนหัว

doctor mŏr   หมอ

dysentery rôhk bìt   โรคบิด

earache bpòo-ut hŏo   ปวดหู

fever kâi   ไข้

filling òot fun   อุดฟัน

first aid gahn bpa-tŏm pa-yah-bahn   การปฐมพยาบาล

flu kâi wùt   ไข้หวัด

fracture	gra-dòok hùk	กระดูกหัก
German measles	rôhk hùt yer-ra-mun	โรคหัดเยอรมัน
glasses	wâirn dtah	แว่นตา
haemorrhage	dtòk lêu-ut	ตกเลือด
hayfever	rôhk hèut	โรคหืด
headache	bpòo-ut hŏo-a	ปวดหัว
heart	hŏo-a jai	หัวใจ
heart attack	hŏo-a jai wai	หัวใจวาย
hepatitis	dtùp ùk-sàyp	ตับอักเสบ
hospital	rohng pa-yah-bahn	โรงพยาบาล
ill	mâi sa-bai	ไม่สบาย
injection	chèet yah	ฉีดยา
itch	kun	คัน
jaundice	rôhk dee-sâhn	โรคดีซ่าน
kidney	tai	ไต
lump	néu-a ngôrk	เนื้องอก
malaria	mah-lay-ree-a	มาเลเรีย
massage	nôo-ut	นวด
measles	rôhk hut	โรคหัด
migraine	bpòo-ut hŏo-a kâhng dee-o	ปวดหัวข้างเดียว
mumps	kahng toom	คางทูม
nausea	ah-gahn klêun hěe-un	อาการคลื่นเหียน
nurse	nahng pa-yah-bahn	นางพยาบาล
operation	gahn pàh dtùt	การผ่าตัด
optician	jùk-sòo pâirt	จักษุแพทย์
pain	kwahm jèp bpòo-ut	ความเจ็บปวด

penicillin	yah pen-ní-seen-lin	ยาเพนนิซีลลิน
plaster *(sticky)*	bpláh-sa-dtêr	ปลาสเตอร์
pneumonia	bpòrt ùk-sàyp	ปอดอักเสบ
prescription	bai sùng yah	ใบสั่งยา
prickly heat	pòt	ผด
rheumatism	rôhk bpòo-ut nai kôr	โรคปวดในข้อ
scratch *(noun)*	roy kòo-un	รอยข่วน
smallpox	kâi tor-ra-pít	ไข้ทรพิษ
sore throat	jèp kor	เจ็บคอ
splint	fèu-uk	เฝือก
splinter	sa-gèt mái	สะเก็ดไม้
sprain	klét	เคล็ด
sting *(verb: insect)*	dtòy	ต่อย
stomach	tórng	ท้อง
stomach ache	bpòo-ut tórng	ปวดท้อง
temperature	bpen kâi	เป็นไข้
tonsils	dtòrm torn-sin	ตอมทอนซิล
toothache	bpòo-ut fun	ปวดฟัน
traditional doctor (herbalist) mǒr pǎirn boh-rahn		หมอแผนโบราณ
traditional medicine	yah pǎirn boh-rahn	ยาแผนโบราณ
travel sickness		
(air)	mao krêu-ung bin	เมาเครื่องบิน
(car)	mao rót	เมารถ
(sea)	mao reu-a	เมาเรือ
ulcer	plǎir gra-pór	แผลกระเพาะ
to vomit	ah-jee-un	อาเจียน

I have a pain in ...
jèp têe ...
เจ็บที่ ...

I do not feel well
róo-sèuk mâi sa-bai
รู้สึกไม่สบาย

I feel faint
róo-sèuk ja bpen lom
รู้สึกจะเป็นลม

I feel sick
róo-sèuk ja ah-jee-un
รู้สึกจะอาเจียน

I feel dizzy
róo-sèuk wee-un hŏo-a
รู้สึกเวียนหัว

It hurts here
jèp dtrong née
เจ็บตรงนี้

It's a sharp pain
jèp bpòo-ut yàhng rairng
เจ็บปวดอย่างแรง

It hurts all the time
jèp dta-lòrt way-lah
เจ็บตลอดเวลา

It only hurts now and then
jèp bpen bahng krúng bahng krao
เจ็บเป็นบางครั้งบางคราว

It stings
sàirp
แสบ

It aches
bpòo-ut
ปวด

I have a temperature
bpen kâi
เป็นไข้

I normally take ...
bpòk-ka-dtì gin yah ...
ปกติกินยา ...

I'm allergic to ...
pǒm (dee-chún) páir ...
ผม (ดิฉัน) แพ้ ...

Have you got anything for ...?
mee yah gâir ... mái?
มียาแก้ ...ไหม

I need a new filling
dtôrng Òot fun mài
ต้องอุดฟันใหม่

THINGS YOU'LL SEE

รถพยาบาล	rót pa-yah bahn	ambulance
คลีนิค	klee-nìk	clinic
ทันตแพทย์	tun-dta-pâirt	dentist

83

ทำฟัน	tum fun	dentist's
นายแพทย์ (น.พ.)	nai pâirt	doctor (male)
แพทย์หญิง (พ.ญ.)	pâirt yǐng	doctor (female)
ตรวจสายตา	dtròo-ut sǎi-dtah	eye test
โรงพยาบาล	rohng pa-yah-bahn	hospital
ฉีดยา	chèet yah	injection
ยา	yah	medicine
ใบสั่งยา	bai sùng yah	prescription
เอ็กซเรย์	'X-ray'	X-ray

THINGS YOU'LL HEAR

rúp-bpra-tahn krúng la ... mét
Take ... pills/tablets at a time

dèum náhm bpai dôo-ay
With water

wun la krúng/sǒrng krúng/sǎhm krúng
Once/twice/three times a day

bpòk-ka-dti rúp-bpra-tahn a-rai?
What do you normally take?

kít wâh koo-un bpai hǎh mǒr
I think you should see a doctor

mâi mee krúp (kâ)
I'm sorry, we don't have that

dtôrng mee bai sùng yah
For that you need a prescription

a *no articles in Thai*

accident OO-bùt-dti-hàyt — อุบัติเหตุ

adaptor krêu-ung bplairng fai fáh — เครื่องแปลงไฟฟ้า

address têe-yòo — ที่อยู่

after lǔng — หลัง

aftershave yah tah lǔng gohn nòo-ut — ยาทาหลังโกนหนวด

again èek — อีก

air-conditioning krêu-ung air — เครื่องแอร์ ,

airport sa-nǎhm bin — สนามบิน

alarm clock nah-li-gah bplòok — นาฬิกาปลุก

alcohol lâo — เหล้า

all túng mòt — ทั้งหมด

  all the streets ta-nǒn túng mòt — ถนนทั้งหมด

  that's all thanks tâo née kòrp-kOOn — เท่านี้ขอบคุณ

almost gèu-up — เกือบ

alone kon dee-o — คนเดียว

already ... láir-o — แล้ว

always sa-měr — เสมอ

America a-may-ri-gah — อเมริกา

American *(adj)* a-may-ri-gun — อเมริกัน

and láir — และ

another *(further)* èek — อีก

  (different) yàhng èun — อย่างอื่น

antibiotics yah bpùti-chee-wa-ná — ยาปฏิชีวนะ

85

antiseptic yah kâh chéu-a   ยาฆ่าเชื้อ
apartment a-páht-mén   อพาร์ตเม้นท์
arm kǎirn   แขน
arrive mah těung   มาถึง
art sǐn-la-bpà   ศิลป
ashtray têe kèe-a bOO-rèe   ที่เขี่ยบุหรี่
asleep: he's asleep káo norn   เขานอนหลับอยู่
lùp yòo
at: at the coffee shop têe kórp-   ที่คอฟฟี่ช็อบ
fêe chórp
attractive sǒo-ay   สวย
aunt: *(elder sister of mother or*   ป้า
father) bpâh
(younger sister of father) ah   อา
(younger sister of mother) náh   น้า
Australia órt-sa-tray-lee-a   ออสเตรเลีย
Australian *(adj)* órt-sa-tray-lee-a   ออสเตรเลีย
awful yâir mâhk   แย่มาก
baby dèk òrn   เด็กอ่อน
back lǔng   หลัง
back street ta-nǒn kâhng nai   ถนนข้างใน
bad mâi dee   ไม่ดี
ball lôok born   ลูกบอล
bamboo mái pài   ไม้ไผ่
bamboo shoot(s) nòr mái   หน่อไม้
banana glôo-ay   กล้วย
band *(music)* wong don-dtree   วงดนตรี
bandage pâh pun plǎir   ผ้าพันแผล

bandit john   โจร
Bangkok grOOng-tâyp   กรุงเทพ ฯ
bank *(money)* ta-nah-kahn   ธนาคาร
bar bah   บาร์
bath àhng àhp náhm   อ่างอาบน้ำ
bathroom hôrng náhm   ห้องน้ำ
battery bair-dta-rêe   แบตเตอรี่
beach chai-hàht   ชายหาด
beans tòo-a   ถั่ว
beard krao   เครา
beautiful *(in appearance)* sŏo-ay   สวย
because prór   เพราะ
bed dtee-ung   เตียง
bedroom hôrng norn   ห้องนอน
beef néu-a woo-a   เนื้อวัว
beer bee-a   เบียร์
before gòrn   ก่อน
beggar kŏr-tahn   ขอทาน
begin rêrm   เริ่ม
behind kâhng lŭng   ข้างหลัง
bell *(large)* ra-kung   ระฆัง
  (small) gra-dìng   กระดิ่ง
  (electrical) grìng   กริ่ง
below dtâi   ใต้
belt *(clothing)* kĕm kùt   เข็มขัด
best dee têe sòOt   ดีที่สุด
better dee gwàh   ดีกว่า
between ra-wàhng   ระหว่าง

bicycle	jùk-gra-yahn	จักรยาน
big	yài	ใหญ่
bikini	bi-gi-nêe	บิกินี่
bill	bin	บิล
birthday	wun gèrt	วันเกิด
happy birthday	sòok sǔn wun gèrt	สุขสรรค์วันเกิด
biscuit	kóok-gêe	คุกกี้
bitter *(taste)*	kǒm	ขม
black	dum	ดำ
blanket	pâh hòm	ผ้าห่ม
blind	dtah bòrt	ตาบอด
blinds	môo-lêe	มู่ลี่
blister	plǎir porng	แผลพอง
blocked *(road, drain)*	dtun	ตัน
blond *(adj)*	pǒm sěe torng	ผมสีทอง
blouse	sêu-a pôo-yǐng	เสื้อผู้หญิง
blue	sěe núm ngern	สีน้ำเงิน
boat	reu-a	เรือ
body	râhng gai	ร่างกาย
boiled rice	kâo sǒo-ay	ข้าวสวย
book *(noun)*	núng-sěu	หนังสือ
bookshop	ráhn kǎi núng-sěu	ร้านขายหนังสือ
boot *(on foot)*	rorng-táo	รองเท้า
border *(of country)*	chai dairn	ชายแดน
boring	nâh bèu-a	น่าเบื่อ
boss	jâo nai	เจ้านาย
both	túng sǒrng	ทั้งสอง

bottle kòo-ut	ขวด
bottle-opener têe bpèrt kòo-ut	ที่เปิดขวด
bowl chahm	ชาม
box hèep	หีบ
boxer núk moo-ay	นักมวย
boy dèk chai	เด็กชาย
boyfriend fairn	แฟน
bra sêu-a yók song	เสื้อยกทรง
bracelet gum-lai meu	กำไลมือ
bread ka-nŏm-bpung	ขนมปัง
breakfast ah-hăhn cháo	อาหารเช้า
bridge sa-pahn	สะพาน
briefcase gra-bpăo	กระเป๋า
British ung-grìt	อังกฤษ
broken dtàirk láir-o	แตกแล้ว
(out of order) sĕe-a	เสีย
brooch kĕm glùt sêu-a	เข็มกลัดเสื้อ
brother: older brother pêe chai	พี่ชาย
younger brother nórng chai	น้องชาย
brown sĕe núm dtahn	สีน้ำตาล
bruise fók-chúm	ฟกช้ำ
brush *(noun)* mái gwàht	ไม้กวาด
Buddha prá-póot-ta-jâo	พระพุทธเจ้า
building ah-kahn	อาคาร
bulb *(elec)* lòrt fai fáh	หลอดไฟฟ้า
bungalow bung-gah-loh	บังกาโล
burglar ka-moy-ee	ขโมย
Burma bpra-tâyt pa-mâh	ประเทศพม่า

burn *(noun)* plǎir mâi — แผลไหม้

bus rót may — รถเมล์

business tóo-rá — ธุระ

businessman núk tóo-rá-gìt — นักธุรกิจ

bus station sa-tǎhn-ee rót may — สถานีรถเมล์

bus stop bpâi rót may — ป้ายรถเมล์

busy *(street)* jor-jair — จอแจ

   (restaurant) nâirn — แน่น

but dtàir — แต่

butter ner-ee sòt — เนยสด

button gra-doom — กระดุม

buy séu — ซื้อ

by: by train/car doy-ee rót fai/ — โดยรถไฟ / รถยนต์
   rót yon

café ráhn gǒo-ay dtĕe-o — ร้านก๋วยเตี๋ยว

cake ka-nǒm káyk — ขนมเค้ก

calculator krêu-ung kít lâyk — เครื่องคิดเลข

call: what is this called? nêe — นี่เรียกว่าอะไร
   rêe-uk wâh a-rai?

Cambodia bpra-tâyt gum-poo-chah — ประเทศกัมพูชา

camera glôrng tài rôop — กล้องถ่ายรูป

can *(tin)* gra-bpǒrng — กระป๋อง

can: can I ...? pǒm (chún) ... — ผม (ฉัน) ... ได้ไหม
   dâi mái?

   can you ...? koon ... dâi mái? — คุณ ... ได้ไหม

   he can't ... káo ... mâi dâi — เขา ... ไม่ได้

Canada bpra-tâyt kair-nah-dah — ประเทศแคนาดา

cap *(hat)* moo-ùk — หมวก

car rót   รถ

card *(business)* bùt   บัตร

careful: be careful ra-wung!   ระวัง

car park têe jòrt rót   ที่จอดรถ

carpet prom   พรม

cash *(money)* ngern sòt   เงินสด

cassette móo-un tâyp kah-set   ม้วนเทปคาสเซ็ท

centre *(of town)* jai glahng   ใจกลาง

chair gâo-êe   เก้าอี้

change *(noun: money)* sàyt sa-dtahng   เศษสตางค์

    (verb: money) lâirk ngern   แลกเงิน

    (verb: clothes, trains) bplèe-un   เปลี่ยน

cheap tòok   ถูก

cheers *(toast)* *nothing said*

cheese ner-ee kǎirng   เนยแข็ง

chemist *(shop)* ráhn kǎi yah   ร้านขายยา

cheque chék   เช็ค

cheque book sa-mòOt chék   สมุดเช็ค

cheque card bùt chék   บัตรเช็ค

chest *(body)* nâh ok   หน้าอก

chewing gum màhk fa-rùng   หมากฝรั่ง

chicken gài   ไก่

child, children dèk   เด็ก

chilli prík   พริก

China bpra-tâyt jeen   ประเทศจีน

chips mun fa-rùng tôrt   มันฝรั่งทอด

chocolate chórk-goh-láirt   ช็อกโกเลต

chopsticks	dta-gèe-up	ตะเกียบ
church	bòht	โบสถ์
cigar	sí-gâh	ซิการ์
cigarette	bOO-rèe	บุหรี่
cinema	rohng nǔng	โรงหนัง
city	meu-ung	เมือง
clean	sa-àht	สะอาด
clever	cha-làht	ฉลาด
clock	nah-li-gah	นาฬิกา
close: to be close *(near)*	glâi	ใกล้
closed	bpìt	ปิด
clothes	sêu-a pâh	เสื้อผ้า
clothes peg	mái nèep pâh	ไม้หนีบผ้า
coast	chai ta-lay	ชายทะเล
coat *(overcoat)*	sêu-a klOOm	เสื้อคลุม
(jacket)	sêu-a nôrk	เสื้อนอก
coathanger	mái kwǎirn sêu-a	ไม้แขวนเสื้อ
cockroach	ma-lairng sàhp	แมลงสาบ
coconut	ma-práo	มะพร้าว
coconut juice	núm ma-práo	น้ำมะพร้าว
coffee	gah-fair	กาแฟ
coffee shop	kórp-fêe chórp	คอฟฟี่ช็อป
cold	yen	เย็น
I have a cold	pǒm (chún) bpen wùt	ผม (ฉัน) เป็นหวัด
colour	sěe	สี
comb *(noun)*	wěe	หวี
come	mah	มา

I come from ... pŏm (chún) mah jàhk ...   ผม (ฉัน) มาจาก ...

come in! chern kâo mah   เชิญเข้ามา

company *(firm)* bor-ri-sùt   บริษัท

complicated sùp sŏn   สับสน

computer korm-pew-dtêr   คอมพิวเตอร์

concert gahn sa-dairng don-dtree   การแสดงดนตรี

condom tŏong yahng   ถุงยาง

constipation tórng pòok   ท้องผูก

consul gong-sŏOn   กงสุล

contact lenses korn-tàirk layn   คอนแทคเลนซ์

cool *(day, weather)* yen   เย็น

corner: on the corner hŏo-a mOOm   หัวมุม

in the corner yòo dtrong hŏo-a mOOm   อยู่ตรงหัวมุม

cost rah-kah   ราคา

what does it cost? rah-kah tâo-rài?   ราคาเท่าไร

cot *(for baby)* bplay   เปล

cotton fãi   ฝ้าย

cotton wool sŭm-lee   สำลี

cough *(verb)* ai   ไอ

country *(nation)* bpra-tâyt   ประเทศ

cousin: my cousin yâht kŏrng pŏm (chún)   ญาติของผม (ฉัน)

crab bpoo   ปู

cramp *(in leg etc)* nèp	เหน็บ
cream kreem	ครีม
credit card bùt kray-dìt	บัตรเครดิต
crisps mun fa-rùng tôrt	มันฝรั่งทอด
crocodile jor-ra-kây	จรเข้
crowd fŏong kon	ฝูงคน
cup tôo-ay	ถ้วย
a cup of coffee gah-fair tôo-ay nèung	กาแฟถ้วยหนึ่ง
curry gairng	แกง
curtains mâhn	ม่าน
Customs sŏOn-la-gah-gorn	ศุลกากร
cut dtùt	ตัด
dangerous un-dta-rai	อันตราย
dark dum	ดำ
daughter lôok săo	ลูกสาว
day wun	วัน
dead dtai	ตาย
deaf hŏo nòo-uk	หูหนวก
dear *(expensive)* pairng	แพง
deep léuk	ลึก
delicious a-ròy	อร่อย
dentist mŏr fun	หมอฟัน
deodorant yah dùp glìn dtoo-a	ยาดับกลิ่นตัว
departure kăh òrk	ขาออก
develop *(films)* láhng	ล้าง
diary sa-mÒOt bun-téuk bpra-jum wun	สมุดบันทึกประจำวัน

dictionary pót-ja-nah-nóo-grom	พจนานุกรม
die dtai	ตาย
different dtàhng	ต่าง
difficult yâhk	ยาก
dinner ah-hăhn yen	อาหารเย็น
dirty sòk-ga-bpròk	สกปรก
disabled pí-gahn	พิการ
disco dit-sa-gôh	ดิสโก้
divorced yàh gun láir-o	หย่ากันแล้ว
do tum	ทำ
doctor mŏr	หมอ
dog măh	หมา
dollar ngern dorn-lâh	เงินดอลลาร์
don't! yàh	อย่า
door bpra-dtoo	ประตู
down: down there yòo têe nôhn	อยู่ที่โน่น
dress *(woman's)* sêu-a chóot	เสื้อชุด
drink *(verb)* dèum	ดื่ม
drinking water náhm dèum	น้ำดื่ม
driving licence bai kùp kèe	ใบขับขี่
drunk mao	เมา
dry hâirng	แห้ง
dry-cleaner ráhn súk-hâirng	ร้านซักแห้ง
durian *(fruit)* tóo-ree-un	ทุเรียน
each dtàir la	แต่ละ
ear hŏo	หู
early *(arrive etc)* ray-o	เร็ว
earring dtôom hŏo	ตุ้มหู

east   dta-wun òrk   ตะวันออก

easy   ngâi   ง่าย

eat   gin kâo   กินข้าว

egg   kài   ไข่

egg noodles   ba-mèe   บะหมี่

either: either ... or ...   ... rĕu ...   .หรือ ....

elastic   sǎi yahng yêut   สายยางยืด

elastic band   yahng rút   ยางรัด

electricity   fai fáh   ไฟฟ้า

elephant   cháhng   ช้าง

else: something else   a-rai èek   อะไรอีก

  somewhere else   têe èun   ที่อื่น

embarrassing   kĕrn   เขิน

embassy   sa-tǎhn tôot   สถานทูต

emergency   chòok chĕrn   ฉุกเฉิน

empty *(vacant)*   wâhng   ว่าง

  (bottle etc)   bplào   เปล่า

end *(verb)*   sîn sòot, jòp   สิ้นสุด , จบ

engaged *(person)*   mûn   หมั้น

  (telephone)   mâi wâhng   ไม่ว่าง

England   bpra-tâyt ung-grìt   ประเทศอังกฤษ

English *(adj)*   ung-grìt   อังกฤษ

  (language)   pah-sǎh ung-grìt   ภาษาอังกฤษ

enough   por   พอ

entrance   tahng kâo   ทางเข้า

envelope   sorng jòt-mǎi   ซองจดหมาย

evening   dtorn glahng keun   ตอนกลางคืน

everyone   tóok kon   ทุกคน

everything tóok yàhng   ทุกอย่าง
everywhere tôo-a bpai   ทั่วไป
excellent yêe-um   เยี่ยม
excuse me *(to get past)* kǒr-tôht   ขอโทษ
   (to get attention) kOOn krúp (ká)   คุณครับ (คะ)
exit tahng òrk   ทางออก
expensive pairng   แพง
eye dtah   ตา
face nâh   หน้า
false teeth fun bplorm   ฟันปลอม
family krôrp-kroo-a   ครอบครัว
fan *(mechanical)* pút lom   พัดลม
   (hand held) pút   พัด
far glai   ไกล
farmer *(of rice)* chao nah   ชาวนา
fashion fair-chûn   แฟชั่น
fast ray-o   เร็ว
fat *(person)* ôo-un   อ้วน
father pôr   พอ
feel róo-sèuk   รู้สึก
   I feel hot pǒm (chún) róo-   ผม (ฉัน) รู้สึกร้อน
   sèuk rórn
ferry reu-a kâhm fâhk   เรือข้ามฟาก
fever kâi   ไข้
few: only a few lék nóy   เล็กน้อย
fiancé(e) kôo mûn   คู่หมั้น
field *(rice, paddy)* nah   นา
film *(cinema)* nǔng   หนัง

(camera) feem	ฟิล์ม
find jer	เจอ
finger néw meu	นิ้วมือ
fire: there's a fire! fai mâi!	ไฟไหม้
fire extinguisher krêu-ung dùp plerng	เครื่องดับเพลิง
first râirk	แรก
fish bplah	ปลา
fisherman kon jùp bplah	คนจับปลา
fishing jùp bplah	จับปลา
fishing boat reu-a bpra-mong	เรือประมง
fizzy sâh	ซ่า
flash *(for camera)* fláirt	แฟลช
flat *(adj)* bairn	แบน
(apartment) flàirt	แฟลต
flavour rót	รส
flea mùt	หมัด
flight têe-o bin	เที่ยวบิน
floating market dta-làht náhm	ตลาดน้ำ
floor *(of room)* péun	พื้น
flower dòrk-mái	ดอกไม้
fly *(verb)* bin	บิน
(insect) ma-lairng wun	แมลงวัน
folk music don-dtree péun meu-ung	ดนตรีพื้นเมือง
food ah-hăhn	อาหาร
food poisoning ah-hăhn bpen pít	อาหารเป็นพิษ
foot táo	เท้า

football fóot-born ฟุตบอล

for: for her sŭm-rùp káo สำหรับเขา

  that's for me nûn sŭm-rùp นั่นสำหรับผม (ฉัน)
  pŏm (chún)

  a bus for ... rót-may bpai ... รถเมล์ไป ...

foreigner chao dtàhng bpra-tâyt ชาวต่างประเทศ

forest bpàh ป่า

fortnight sŏrng ah-tít สองอาทิตย์

free free ฟรี

freezer dtôo châir kăirng ตู้แช่แข็ง

fridge dtôo yen ตู้เย็น

fried rice kâo pùt ข้าวผัด

friend pêu-un เพื่อน

friendly bpen mít เป็นมิตร

frog gòp กบ

from jàhk จาก

front nâh หน้า

fruit pŏn-la-mái ผลไม้

fruit juice núm pŏn-la-mái น้ำผลไม้

fry *(deep fry)* tôrt ทอด

  (stir fry) pùt ผัด

full dtem láir-o เต็มแล้ว

  I'm full pŏm (chún) ìm láir-o ผม (ฉัน)อิ่มแล้ว

funny *(strange)* bplàirk แปลก

  (amusing) dta-lòk ตลก

garden sŏo-un สวน

garlic gra-tee-um กระเทียม

gay *(homosexual)* gra-ter-ee กระเทย

gents *(toilet)* hôrng náhm pôo-chai   ห้องน้ำผู้ชาย
get *(fetch)* ao ... mah   เอา ... มา
   (obtain) dâi   ได้
   (train, bus etc) kêun   ขึ้น
   have you got ...? mee ... mái?   มี ... ไหม
get in *(to car)* kêun   ขึ้น
   (arrive) mah tĕung   มาถึง
get up *(in morning)* dtèun   ตื่น
girl pôo-yĭng   ผู้หญิง
girlfriend fairn   แฟน
give hâi   ให้
glad yin dee   ยินดี
glass gâir-o   แก้ว
glasses *(spectacles)* wâirn dtah   แว่นตา
glue gao   กาว
go bpai   ไป
gold torng   ทอง
Golden Triangle săhm lèe-um   สามเหลี่ยมทองคำ
   torng kum
goldsmith châhng torng   ช่างทอง
good dee   ดี
goodbye lah gòrn ná   ลากอนนะ
government rút-ta-bahn   รัฐบาล
granddaughter lăhn săo   หลานสาว
grandfather *(paternal)* bpòo   ปู่
   (maternal) dtah   ตา
grandmother *(paternal)* yâh   ย่า
   (maternal) yai   ยาย

grandson lăhn chai หลานชาย

grapes a-ngÒOn องุ่น

grass yâh หญ้า

great: that's great! yôrt! ยอด

Great Britain bpra-tâyt ung-grìt ประเทศอังกฤษ

green sěe kěe-o สีเขียว

grey sěe tao สีเทา

ground floor chún nèung ชั้นหนึ่ง

guide *(noun)* múk-kOO-tâyt มัคคุเทศก์

guidebook kôo meu num têe-o คู่มือนำเที่ยว

gun bpeun ปืน

hair pǒm ผม

hairdryer krêu-ung bpào pǒm เครื่องเป่าผม

half krêung ครึ่ง

ham mǒo hairm หมูแฮม

hamburger hairm-ber-gêr แฮมเบอร์เกอร์

hammer kórn ค้อน

hand meu มือ

handbag gra-bpǎo těu กระเป๋าถือ

handkerchief pâh chét nâh ผ้าเช็ดหน้า

handle *(noun)* dâhm ด้าม

handsome rôop lòr รูปหล่อ

hangover bpÒo-ut hǒo-a ปวดหัว

happy dee jai ดีใจ

harbour tâh reu-a ท่าเรือ

hard kǎirng แข็ง

 (difficult) yâhk ยาก

hat mòo-uk หมวก

have mee · มี
  do you have ...? mee ... mái? · มี ... ไหม
  I don't have ... pŏm (chún) · ผม (ฉัน) ไม่มี ...
  mâi mee ...

hay fever rôhk hèut · โรคหืด

he káo · เขา

head hŏo-a · หัว

headache bpòo-ut hŏo-a · ปวดหัว

headlights fai nâh rót · ไฟหน้ารถ

hear dâi yin · ได้ยิน

hearing aid krêu-ung chôo-ay fung · เครื่องช่วยฟัง

heart hŏo-a jai · หัวใจ

heat kwahm rórn · ความร้อน

heavy nùk · หนัก

heel (*foot*) sôn táo · ส้นเท้า
  (*shoe*) sôn rorng táo · ส้นรองเท้า

hello (*by man*) sa-wùt dee krúp · สวัสดีครับ
  (*by woman*) sa-wùt dee kâ · สวัสดีค่ะ

help (*verb*) chôo-ay · ช่วย
  help! chôo-ay dôo-ay! · ช่วยด้วย !

her káo · เขา
  her ... ... kŏrng káo · ...ของเขา

here têe nêe · ที่นี่

hers kŏrng káo · ของเขา

hi! bpai nǎi? · ไปไหน

high sŏong · สูง

hill kǎo · เขา

hill tribe chao kǎo · ชาวเขา

him káo   เขา

hire châo   เช่า

his ... ... kŏrng káo   ... ของเขา

holiday wun yòot   วันหยุด

horrible yâir mâhk   แย่มาก

hostess *(in bar)* pôo-yĭng bah   ผู้หญิงบาร์

hot rórn   ร้อน

  (with spices) pèt   เผ็ด

hotel rohng rairm   โรงแรม

house bâhn   บ้าน

how: how ...? ... yung ngai?   ... อย่างไร

hungry: I'm hungry pŏm   ผม (ฉัน) หิว
  (chún) hĕw

hurry: I'm in a hurry pŏm   ผม(ฉัน)ต้องรีบ
  (chún) dtôrng rêep

husband săh-mee   สามี

I *(male)* pŏm   ผม

  (female) dee-chún, chún   ดิฉัน,ฉัน

ice núm kăirng   น้ำแข็ง

ice cream ai-sa-kreem   ไอศครีม

if tâh   ถ้า

ill mâi sa-bai   ไม่สบาย

immediately tun-tee   ทันที

impossible bpen bpai mâi dâi เป็นไปไม่ได้

in nai   ใน

  in English bpen pah-săh ung-grìt เป็นภาษาอังกฤษ

India bpra-tâyt in-dee-a   ประเทศอินเดีย

infection ah-gahn ùk-sàyp   อาการอักเสบ

103

information kào săhn   ข่าวสาร
insect repellent yah gun ma-lairng   ยากันแมลง
insurance bpra-gun   ประกัน
interesting nâh sŏn jai   น่าสนใจ
interpret bplair   แปล
Ireland ai-lairn   ไอร์แลนด์
iron *(for clothes)* dtao rêet   เตารีด
island gòr   เกาะ
it mun   มัน
  it's expensive (mun) pairng   (มัน)แพง
jack *(for car)* mâir rairng   แม่แรง
jacket sêu-a nôrk   เสื้อนอก
jeans yeen   ยีนส์
jellyfish mairng ga-prOOn   แมงกะพรุน
jewellery pét ploy   เพชรพลอย
job ngahn   งาน
journey gahn dern tahng   การเดินทาง
jug yèu-uk   เหยือก
jumper sêu-a sa-wét-dtêr   เสื้อเสวตเตอร์
jungle bpàh   ป่า
just *(only)* tâo-nún   เท่านั้น
  just one un dee-o tâo-nún   อันเดียวเท่านั้น
key gOOn-jair   กุญแจ
kilo gi-loh   กิโล
kilometre gi-loh-mét   กิโลเมตร
kitchen hôrng kroo-a   ห้องครัว
knee hŏo-a kào   หัวเข่า
knife mêet   มีด

know: I don't know   pŏm   ผม (ฉัน) ไม่รู้
  (chún) mâi róo

ladies *(toilet)*   hôrng náhm pôo-yĭng   ห้องน้ำผู้หญิง

lady   sOO-pâhp sa-dtree   สุภาพสตรี

lake   ta-lay sàhp   ทะเลสาบ

lane *(narrow street)*   soy   ซอย

Laos   bpra-tâyt lao   ประเทศลาว

large   yài   ใหญ่

last *(previous)*   têe láir-o   ที่แล้ว
   (final)   sòOt-tái   สุดท้าย

  last year   bpee têe láir-o   ปีที่แล้ว

late *(at night)*   dèuk   ดึก
   (behind schedule)   cháh   ช้า

later   tee lŭng   ทีหลัง

laxative   yah tài   ยาถ่าย

left *(not right)*   sái   ซ้าย

left luggage   têe fàhk gra-bpăo   ที่ฝากกระเป๋า

leg   kăh   ขา

lemon   ma-nao   มะนาว

lemonade   núm ma-nao   น้ำมะนาว

letter *(in mail)*   jòt-măi   จดหมาย

letterbox   dtôo jòt-măi   ตู้จดหมาย

lettuce   pùk-gàht   ผักกาด

library   hôrng sa-mòOt   ห้องสมุด

life   chee-wít   ชีวิต

lift *(in hotel etc)*   líf   ลิฟท์

  could you give me a lift?   ช่วยไปส่งหน่อยได้ไหม
  chôo-ay bpai sòng nòy, dâi mái?

light *(noun)* fai   ไฟ

  (not heavy) bao   เบา

lighter *(cigarette)* fai cháirk   ไฟแช็ก

like: I'd like a ... pǒm (chún) ao ...   ผม (ฉัน) เอา ...

  I like you pǒm (chún) chôrp kOOn   ผม (ฉัน) ชอบคุณ

  one like that měu-un un nún   เหมือนอันนั้น

lipstick líp sa-dtík   ลิปสติก

litre lít   ลิตร

little lék   เล็ก

  just a little nít dee-o tâo-nún   นิดเดียวเท่านั้น

liver dtùp   ตับ

lobster gôong gâhm grahm   กุ้งก้ามกราม

long yao   ยาว

  how long does it take? chái way-lah nahn tâo-rài?   ใช้เวลานานเท่าไร

lose: I've lost my ... ... kǒrng pǒm (chún) hǎi   ...ของผม(ฉัน)หาย

lot: a lot mâhk   มาก

  a lot of money ngern mâhk   เงินมาก

loud dung   ดัง

love: I love you chún rúk ter   ฉันรักเธอ

lovely yêe-um ler-ee   เยี่ยมเลย

low dtùm   ต่ำ

luck chôhk   โชค

  good luck! chôhk dee!   โชคดี !

luggage gra-bpǎo   กระเป๋า

lunch ah-hăhn glahng wun	อาหารกลางวัน
mail jòt-măi	จดหมาย
make tum	ทำ
make-up krêu-ung sŭm-ahng	เครื่องสำอาง
man pôo-chai	ผู้ชาย
manager pôo-jùt-gahn	ผู้จัดการ
mango ma-môo-ung	มะม่วง
map păirn-têe	แผนที่
market dta-làht	ตลาด
married: I'm married pŏm (chún) dtàirng ngahn láir-o	ผม (ฉัน)แต่งงานแล้ว
massage nôo-ut	นวด
matches mái kèet	ไม้ขีด
material *(cloth)* pâh	ผ้า
me *(male)* pŏm	ผม
(female) dee-chún, chún	ดิฉัน , ฉัน
it's for me sŭm-rùp pŏm (chún)	สำหรับผม (ฉัน)
medicine yah	ยา
meeting bpra-chOOm	ประชุม
melon: water melon dtairng moh	แตงโม
musk melon dtairng tai	แตงไทย
metre máyt	เมตร
midday: at midday têe-ung wun	เที่ยงวัน
middle: in the middle yòo dtrong glahng	อยู่ตรงกลาง
midnight: at midnight têe-ung keun	เที่ยงคืน

mile	mai	ไมล์
milk	nom	นม
mine	kŏrng pŏm (chún)	ของผม (ฉัน)
mineral water	núm râir	น้ำแร่
mirror	gra-jòk ngao	กระจกเงา
Miss	nahng-săo	นางสาว
mistake	kwahm pìt	ความผิด
monastery	wút	วัด
money	ngern	เงิน
monk	prá	พระ
monsoon	mor-ra-sŏOm	มรสุม
month	deu-un	เดือน
moon	prá-jun	พระจันทร์
more	gwàh	กว่า
more than	mâhk gwàh	มากกว่า
morning	cháo	เช้า
mosquito	yOOng	ยุง
mosquito net	mÓOng	มุ้ง
mother	mâir	แม่
motorbike	rót mor-dter-sai	รถมอร์เตอร์ไซค์
mountain	poo-kăo	ภูเขา
moustache	nòo-ut	หนวด
mouth	bpàhk	ปาก
Mr	nai	นาย
Mrs	nahng	นาง
much	mâhk	มาก
much better	dee kêun mâhk	ดีขึ้นมาก
museum	pí-pít-ta-pun	พิพิธภัณฑ์

mushroom hèt   เห็ด

music don-dtree   ดนตรี

must: I must ... pŏm (chún)   ผม (ฉัน) ต้อง ...
 dtôrng ...

my ... ... kŏrng pŏm (chún)   ...ของผม (ฉัน)

narrow *(road)* kâirp   แคบ

near glâi   ใกล้

  is it near here? yòo glâi mái?   อยู่ใกล้ไหม

necessary jum-bpen   จำเป็น

necklace sôy kor   สร้อยคอ

need: I need a ... pŏm (chún)   ผม (ฉัน) ต้องการ ...
 dtôrng-gahn ...

needle kĕm   เข็ม

nephew lăhn chai   หลานชาย

never mâi ker-ee   ไม่เคย

new mài   ใหม่

news kào   ข่าว

newspaper núng-sĕu pim   หนังสือพิมพ์

New Zealand bpra-tâyt new see- ประเทศนิวซีแลนด์
 láirn

next ... ... nâh   ...หน้า

  next to dtìt gùp   ติดกับ

nice *(person, weather)* dee   ดี

  (meal) a-ròy   อร่อย

  (town) sŏo-ay   สวย

niece lăhn săo   หลานสาว

night glahng keun   กลางคืน

  for one night keun dee-o   คืนเดียว

109

night club náit klúp   ไนท์คลับ

no: I've no money pǒm (chún)   ผม (ฉัน) ไม่มีเงิน
  mâi mee ngern

noisy nòo-uk hǒo   หนวกหู

noodles gǒo-ay dtěe-o   ก๋วยเตี๋ยว

  fried noodles pùt tai   ผัดไทย

noodle shop ráhn gǒo-ay dtěe-o   ร้านก๋วยเตี๋ยว

north něu-a   เหนือ

nose ja-mòok   จมูก

not mâi   ไม่

  not for me mâi châi sǔm-rùp   ไม่ใช่สำหรับผม (ฉัน)
  pǒm (chún)

nothing mâi mee a-rai   ไม่มีอะไร

now děe-o née   เดี๋ยวนี้

number *(figure)* mǎi lâyk   หมายเลข

  (of room) ber hôrng   เบอร์ห้อง

  (telephone) ber toh-ra-sùp   เบอร์โทรศัพท์

of kǒrng   ของ

  the name of the hotel chêu   ชื่อของโรงแรม
  kǒrng rohng rairm

office têe tum ngahn   ที่ทำงาน

often bòy bòy   บ่อย ๆ

oil *(motor)* núm mun krêu-ung   น้ำมันเครื่อง

  (vegetable) núm mun pêut   น้ำมันพืช

OK oh-kay   โอเค

old *(things)* gào   เก่า

  (people) gàir   แก่

on bon   บน

on the roof bon lŭng-kah   บนหลังคา

on the·beach chai ta-lay   ชายทะเล

one nèung   หนึ่ง

that one un nún   อันนั้น

onion hǒo-a hǒrm   หัวหอม

only ... ...tâo-nún   ... เท่านั้น

open *(adj)* bpèrt   เปิด

opposite: opposite the temple dtrong kâhm wút   ตรงข้ามวัด

or rěu   หรือ

orange *(fruit)* sôm   ส้ม

(colour) sěe sôm   สีส้ม

orange juice núm sôm   น้ำส้ม

other: the other ... èek ... nèung   อีก ... หนึ่ง

our(s) ... ... kǒrng rao   ...ของเรา

out: he's out káo mâi yòo   เขาไม่อยู่

outside kâhng nôrk   ข้างนอก

over: over there têe nôhn   ที่โน่น

oyster hǒy nahng rom   หอยนางรม

packet sorng   ซอง

paddy field nah   นา

page *(of book)* nâh   หน้า

pair kôo   คู่

paper gra-dàht   กระดาษ

parcel hòr   ห่อ

pardon? a-rai ná?   อะไรนะ

parents pôr-mâir   พ่อแม่

park *(noun)* sǒo-un sǎh-tah-ra-ná   สวนสาธารณะ

(verb) jòrt	จอด
party *(group)* glòom kon	กลุ่มคน
(celebration) ngahn lée-ung	งานเลี้ยง
passport núng-sěu dern tahng	หนังสือเดินทาง
path tahng	ทาง
pavement bàht wít-těe	บาทวิถี
pay *(verb)* jài	จ่าย
can I pay, please? chôo-ay gèp dtung nòy	ช่วยเก็บสตางค์หน่อย
pen bpàhk-gah	ปากกา
pencil din-sŏr	ดินสอ
penknife mêet púp	มีดพับ
people kon	คน
pepper *(spice)* prík tai	พริกไทย
green pepper prík yòo-uk	พริกหยวก
red pepper prík yòo-uk dairng	พริกหยวกแดง
per: ... per night keun la ...	คืนละ ...
perfume núm hŏrm	น้ำหอม
perhaps bahng tee	บางที
perm dùt pŏm	ดัดผม
person kon	คน
petrol núm mun	น้ำมัน
petrol station púm núm mun	ปั๊มน้ำมัน
photograph *(noun)* rôop tài	รูปถ่าย
(verb) tài rôop	ถ่ายรูป
photographer châhng tài rôop	ช่างถ่ายรูป
phrasebook kôo meu sŏn-ta-nah	คู่มือสนทนา

pickpocket ka-moy-ee lóo-ung gra-bpǎo   ขโมยล้วงกระเป๋า

picture rôop   รูป

piece chín   ชิ้น

  a piece of ... ... chín nèung   ...ชิ้นหนึ่ง

pillow mǒrn   หมอน

pin *(noun)* kěm mòOt   เข็มหมุด

pineapple sùp-bpa-rót   สับปะรด

pink sěe chom-poo   สีชมพู

pipe *(smoking)* glôrng yah sòop   กล้องยาสูบ

  (water) tôr náhm   ท่อน้ำ

place *(noun)* sa-tǎhn-têe   สถานที่

plane krêu-ung bin   เครื่องบิน

plant dtôn mái   ต้นไม้

plastic bag tǒOng bplah-sa-tìk   ถุงปลาสติก

plate jahn   จาน

play *(in theatre)* la-korn   ละคร

please: yes please dee see krúp (kâ)   ดีซีครับ (คะ)

  could you please ...? chôo-ay ... nòy dâi mái?   ช่วย ... หน่อยได้ไหม

plug bplúk   ปลั๊ก

  (for car) hǒo-a tee-un   หัวเทียน

pocket gra-bpǎo   กระเป๋า

poisonous bpen pít   เป็นพิษ

policeman dtum ròo-ut   ตำรวจ

polite sOO-pâhp   สุภาพ

pool *(for swimming)* sà wâi náhm สระว่ายน้ำ

poor *(not rich)* jon	จน
pop music playng bpórp	เพลงป๊อบ
pork néu-a mŏo	เนื้อหมู
porter *(hotel)* kon fâo bpra-dtoo	คนเฝ้าประตู
(*station etc*) pa-núk ngahn rót fai	พนักงานรถไฟ
possible bpen bpai dâi	เป็นไปได้
post *(noun: mail)* jòt-măi	จดหมาย
postbox dtôo bprai-sa-nee	ตู้ไปรษณีย์
postcard bpóht-káht	โปสการ์ด
post office bprai-sa-nee	ไปรษณีย์
potato mun fa-rùng	มันฝรั่ง
pound *(money)* bporn	ปอนด์
prawns gôOng	กุ้ง
pregnant mee tórng	มีท้อง
present *(gift)* kŏrng kwŭn	ของขวัญ
pretty sŏo-ay	สวย
price rah-kah	ราคา
priest prá	พระ
problem bpun-hăh	ปัญหา
prostitute sŏh-pay-nee	โสเภณี
pull deung	ดึง
puncture yahng dtàirk	ยางแตก
purse gra-bpăo sa-dtahng	กระเป๋าสตางค์
push plùk	ผลัก
pyjamas sêu-a gahng-gayng norn	เสื้อกางเกงนอน
question kum tăhm	คำถาม
queue *(noun)* kew	คิว
quick ray-o	เร็ว

quiet *(place, hotel)* ngêe-up   เงียบ
quite: quite a lot mâhk por   มากพอสมควร
  sŏm-koo-un
radiator môr náhm   หม้อน้ำ
radio wít-ta-yóo   วิทยุ
railway tahng rót fai   ทางรถไฟ
rain *(noun)* fŏn   ฝน
  it's raining fŏn dtòk   ฝนตก
rainy season nâh fŏn   หน้าฝน
rat nŏo   หนู
razor mêet gohn   มีดโกน
razor blades bai mêet gohn   ใบมีดโกน
read àhn   อ่าน
ready *(finished)* sèt   เสร็จ
receipt bai sèt rúp ngern   ใบเสร็จรับเงิน
record *(music)* jahn sĕe-ung   จานเสียง
red sĕe dairng   สีแดง
religion săh-sa-năh   ศาสนา
rent *(for room etc)* kâh châo   ค่าเช่า
  (verb: car etc) châo   เช่า
repair *(verb)* sôrm   ซ่อม
reserve jorng   จอง
restaurant ráhn ah-hăhn   ร้านอาหาร
return *(come back)* glùp   กลับ
  (give back) keun hâi   คืนให้
return ticket dtŏo-a bpai-   ตั๋วไปกลับ
  glùp
rice kâo   ข้าว

rice field nah   นา
rich *(person)* roo-ay   รวย
right *(correct)* tòok   ถูก
  (not left) kwăh   ขวา
ring *(on finger)* wăirn   แหวน
river mâir náhm   แม่น้ำ
road ta-nŏn   ถนน
roof lŭng-kah   หลังคา
room hôrng   ห้อง
  (space) têe wâhng   ที่ว่าง
rope chêu-uk   เชือก
round *(adj)* glom   กลม
rubber *(material)* yahng   ยาง
  (eraser) yahng lóp   ยางลบ
rubbish *(waste)* ka-yà   ขยะ
  (poor quality) mâi ao năi   ไม่เอาไหน
rucksack bpây lŭng   เป้หลัง
ruins sâhk sa-lùk hùk pung   ซากสลักหักพัง
run *(person)* wîng   วิ่ง
sad sâo   เศร้า
safe *(not in danger)* bplòrt-pai   ปลอดภัย
  (not dangerous) mâi un-dta-rai   ไม่อันตราย
safety pin kĕm glùt   เข็มกลัด
salad sa-lùt   สลัด
salt gleu-a   เกลือ
same mĕu-un gun   เหมือนกัน
  the same again, please kŏr   ขออย่างเดิม
  yàhng derm

sand sai   ทราย

sandal(s) rorng táo dtàir   รองเท้าแตะ

sandwich sairn-wít   แซนด์วิช

sanitary towels pâh a-nah-mai   ผ้าอนามัย

sauce núm jîm   น้ำจิ้ม

sausage sâi gròrk   ไส้กรอก

say: how do you say ... in   ... ภาษาไทยพูดว่าอย่างไร
  Thai? ... pahsăh tai pôot wâh
  yung-ngai?

school rohng ree-un   โรงเรียน

scissors dta-grai   ตะไกร

Scotland bpra-tâyt sa-górt-lairn   ประเทศสกอตแลนด์

screwdriver kăi koo-ung   ไขควง

sea ta-lay   ทะเล

seafood ah-hăhn ta-lay   อาหารทะเล

seat têe nûng   ที่นั่ง

seat belt kĕm kùt ni-ra-pai   เข็มขัดนิรภัย

second *(in series)* têe sŏrng   ที่สอง
  (of time) wí-nah-tee   วินาที

see hĕn   เห็น
  I see! kâo jai láir-o   เข้าใจแล้ว

sell kăi   ขาย

sellotape *(R)* sa-górt táyp   สก๊อตเทป

separately *(pay, travel)* yâirk gun   แยกกัน

shade: in the shade nai rôm   ในร่ม

shampoo yah sà pŏm   ยาสระผม

shark bplah cha-lăhm   ปลาฉลาม

shave gohn   โกน

shaving foam   kreem gohn nòo-ut   ครีมโกนหนวด

she   káo   เขา

sheet *(for bed)*   pâh bpoo têe norn   ผ้าปูที่นอน

ship   reu-a   เรือ

shirt   sêu-a chért   เสื้อเชิ้ต

shoe   rorng táo   รองเท้า

shoelaces   chêu-uk pòok rorng táo   เชือกผูกรองเท้า

shop   ráhn   ร้าน

short *(in length)*   sûn   สั้น
    (person)   dtêe-a   เตี้ย

shorts   gahng-gayng kăh sûn   กางเกงขาสั้น

shoulder   lài   ไหล่

shower *(in bathroom)*   fùk boo-a   ฝักบัว

shrimps   gÔOng   กุ้ง

shut *(verb)*   bpìt   ปิด

shutter *(on window)*   sa-lùk   สลักหน้าต่าง
    nâh-dtàhng

side street   soy   ซอย

sight: the sights of ...   sa-tăhn-   สถานที่น่าเที่ยวใน ...
    têe nâh têe-o nai ...

silk   măi   ไหม

silver   ngern   เงิน

sing   rórng playng   ร้องเพลง

single: I'm single   pŏm (chún)   ผม (ฉัน) เป็นโสด
    bpen sòht

sister: older sister   pêe săo   พี่สาว
    younger sister   nórng săo   น้องสาว

sit   nûng   นั่ง

skirt gra-bprohng	กระโปรง
sky fáh	ฟ้า
sleep norn lùp	นอนหลับ
slow cháh	ช้า
slowly cháh cháh	ช้า ๆ
small lék	เล็ก
smell (*have bad smell*) měn	เหม็น
smile (*verb*) yím	ยิ้ม
smoke (*noun*) kwun	ควัน
do you smoke? kOOn sòop	คุณสูบบุหรี่ไหม
bOO-rèe mái?	
snake ngoo	งู
so: so good dee jing	ดีจริง
not so much mâi mâhk tâo-rài	ไม่มากเท่าไร
soap sa-bòo	สบู่
sock tŏOng-táo	ถุงเท้า
soft (*material etc*) nîm	นิ่ม
soft drink náhm kòo-ut	น้ำขวด
sole (*of shoes*) péun rorng táo	พื้นรองเท้า
somebody krai	ใคร
something a-rai	อะไร
sometimes bahng tee	บางที
somewhere têe nǎi	ที่ไหน
son lôok chai	ลูกชาย
song playng	เพลง
soon děe-o	เดี๋ยว
sorry kŏr-tôht	ขอโทษ
sorry? a-rai ná krúp (ká)?	อะไรนะครับ (คะ)

soup sóOp	ซุป
south dtâi	ใต้
souvenir kŏrng têe ra-léuk	ของที่ระลึก
soy sauce núm see éw	น้ำซีอิ๊ว
spanner gOOn-jair bpàhk dtai	กุญแจปากตาย
speak pôot	พูด
spider mairng mOOm	แมงมุม
spoon chórn	ช้อน
spring *(season)* reu-doo bai mái plì	ฤดูใบไม้ผลิ
squid bplah-mèuk	ปลาหมึก
stairs bun-dai	บันได
stamp *(for letter)* sa-dtairm	แสตมป์
start *(verb)* rêrm	เริ่ม
station *(railway)* sa-tăhn-nee rót fai	สถานีรถไฟ
steak néu-a sa-dték	เนื้อเสต๊ก
steal: my bag has been stolen gra-bpăo tòok ka-moy-ee	กระเป๋าถูกขโมย
stewardess "air hostess"	แอร์โฮสเตส
sticking plaster bplah-sa-dter	ปลาสเตอร์
sticky rice kâo nĕe-o	ข้าวเหนียว
stockings tŏOng nôrng	ถุงน่อง
stomach tórng	ท้อง
stop *(bus stop)* bpâi rót-may	ป้ายรถเมล์
stop here yÒOt têe nêe	หยุดที่นี่
storm pah-yÓO	พายุ
straight: it's straight ahead yòo dtrong nâh	อยู่ตรงหน้า

street ta-nŏn   ถนน
string chêu-uk   เชือก
student núk sèuk-săh   นักศึกษา
stupid ngôh   โง่
sugar núm dtahn   น้ำตาล
suit *(noun)* chóot   ชุด
suitcase gra-bpăo dern tahng   กระเป๋าเดินทาง
sun prá-ah-tít   พระอาทิตย์
sunblock *(cream)* yah tah gun ยาทากันแดด
  dàirt
sunburnt tòok dàirt   ถูกแดด
sunglasses wâirn gun dàirt   แว่นกันแดด
sunshade ngao dàirt   เงาแดด
sunstroke rôhk páir dàirt   โรคแพ้แดด
suntan pěw klúm dàirt   ผิวคล้ำแดด
suntan lotion kreem tah àhp   ครีมทาอาบแดด
  dàirt
supermarket sóop-bpêr-mah-gêt ซุปเปอร์มาร์เก็ต
sure: I'm sure pŏm (chún)   ผม (ฉัน) แน่ใจ
  nâir jai
  are you sure? koon nâir jai   คุณแน่ใจหรือ
  rĕu?
surname nahm sa-gOOn   นามสกุล
sweat *(noun)* ngèu-a   เหงื่อ
  (verb) ngèu-a òrk   เหงื่อออก
sweet *(taste)* wăhn   หวาน
sweet and sour bprêe-o wăhn   เปรี้ยวหวาน
sweets tórp-fêe   ทอฟฟี่ ·

sweltering: it's sweltering   rórn   ร้อนเป็นบ้า
  bpen bâh

swim *(verb)*   wâi náhm   ว่ายน้ำ

swimming costume   chóot àhp   ชุดอาบน้ำ
  náhm

swimming pool   sà wâi náhm   สระว่ายน้ำ

swimming trunks   gahng gayng   กางเกงว่ายน้ำ
  wâi náhm

swollen   boo-um   บวม

table   dtó   โต๊ะ

take *(something somewhere)*   เอา ...ไป
  ao ... bpai

  (someone somewhere)   pah ...   พา ... ไป
  bpai

talk *(verb)*   pôot   พูด

tall   sŏong   สูง

tampons   tairm-porn   แทมพอน

tap   górk náhm   ก๊อกน้ำ

tape   táyp   เทป

taxi   táirk-sêe   แท็กซี่

tea   núm chah   น้ำชา

telegram   toh-ra-lâyk   โทรเลข

telephone   toh-ra-sùp   โทรศัพท์

television   toh-ra-tút   โทรทัศน์

temperature   OOn-ha-poom   อุณหภูมิ
  (fever)   kâi   ไข้

temple *(religious)*   wút   วัด

tent   tén   เต็นท์

terrible yâir mâhk   แย่มาก
Thai *(adj)* tai   ไทย
  (language) pah-săh tai   ภาษาไทย
Thailand *(formal)* bpra-tâyt tai   ประเทศไทย
  (informal) meu-ung tai   เมืองไทย
than gwàh   กว่า
  smaller than ... lék gwàh ...   เล็กกว่า ...
thanks, thank you kòrp-kOOn   ขอบคุณ
that: that woman pôo-yĭng kon   ผู้หญิงคนนั้น
  nún
  that man pôo chai kon nún   ผู้ชายคนนั้น
  what's that? nûn a-rai?   นั่นอะไร
the *no articles in Thai*
theatre rohng la-korn   โรงละคร
their ... ... kŏrng káo   ...ของเขา
theirs kŏrng káo   ของเขา
them káo   เขา
then *(after that)* lŭng jàhk nún   หลังจากนั้น
  (at that time) way-lah nún   เวลานั้น
there têe-nûn   ที่นั่น
  is/are there ...? mee ... mái?   มี ... ไหม
  there is/are ... mee ...   มี ...
  there isn't/ aren't ... mâi mee ... ไม่มี ...
these pôo-uk née   พวกนี้
they *(people)* káo   เขา
  (things) mun   มัน
thick năh   หนา
thin bahng   บาง

thing kǒrng	ของ	
think kít	คิด	
thirsty: I'm thirsty pǒm (chún) hěw náhm	ผม (ฉัน) หิวน้ำ	
this: this street ta-nǒn née	ถนนนี้	
this one un née	อันนี้	
what's this? nêe a-rai?	นี่อะไร	
those pôo-uk nún	พวกนั้น	
throat kor	คอ	
through pàhn	ผ่าน	
thunderstorm pah-yóo fǒn	พายุฝน	
ticket dtǒo-a	ตั๋ว	
tie *(around neck)* nék-tai	เน็คไท	
tights tǒong yai boo-a	ถุงใยบัว	
time way-lah	เวลา	
what's the time? gèe mohng láir-o?	กี่โมงแล้ว	
next time krao nâh	คราวหน้า	
timetable dtah-rahng way-lah	ตารางเวลา	
tin *(can)* gra-bpǒrng	กระป๋อง	
tin-opener têe bpèrt gra-bpǒrng	ที่เปิดกระป๋อง	
tip *(money)* ngern típ	เงินทิป	
tired nèu-ay	เหนื่อย	
tissues pâh chét meu	ผ้าเช็ดมือ	
to: to England bpai ung-grìt	ไปอังกฤษ	
toast *(bread)* ka-nǒm bpung bpîng	ขนมปังปิ้ง	
toasted bananas glôo-ay bpîng	กล้วยปิ้ง	
today wun née	วันนี้	

together dôo-ay gun   ด้วยกัน

toilet hôrng náhm   ห้องน้ำ

toilet paper gra-dàht chum-rá   กระดาษชำระ

tomato ma-kěu-a tâyt   มะเขือเทศ

tomato juice núm ma-kěu-a tâyt   น้ำมะเขือเทศ

tomorrow prôOng née   พรุ่งนี้

tonic (water) núm toh-ník   น้ำโทนิค

tonight keun née   คืนนี้

too (excessively) ... ... gern bpai   ...เกินไป
  (also) ... dôo-ay   ... ด้วย

tooth fun   ฟัน

toothbrush bprairng sěe fun   แปรงสีฟัน

toothpaste yah sěe fun   ยาสีฟัน

torch fai chǎi   ไฟฉาย

tour (noun) rai-gahn num têe-o   รายการนำเที่ยว

tourist núk tôrng têe-o   นักท่องเที่ยว

tourist office sǔm-núk kào sǎhn   สำนักข่าวสารนักท่องเที่ยว
  núk tôrng têe-o

towel pâh chét dtoo-a   ผ้าเช็ดตัว

town meu-ung   เมือง

traffic lights fai sǔn-yahn ja-   ไฟสัญญาณจราจร
  rah-jorn

train rót fai   รถไฟ

translate bplair   แปล

travel agent "travel agent"   ทราเวิลเอเยนต์

traveller's cheque chék dern   เช็คเดินทาง
  tahng

tree dtôn mái   ต้นไม้

trousers gahng-gayng	กางเกง
try *(try out, test)* lorng	ลอง
T-shirt sêu-a yêut	เสื้อยืด
tweezers bpàhk kêep	ปากคีบ
tyre yahng rót	ยางรถ
umbrella rôm	ร่ม
uncle *(older brother of father or mother)* lOOng	ลุง
(younger brother of father) ah	อา
(younger brother of mother) náh	น้า
under *(spatially)* dtâi	ใต้
vaccination chéet wúk seen	ฉีดวัคซีน
vanilla wá-ní-lah	วานิลา
vase jair-gun	แจกัน
vegetables pùk	ผัก
vegetarian mâi gin néu-a	ไม่กินเนื้อ
very ... ... mâhk	...มาก
village mòo-bâhn	หมู่บ้าน
visa wee-sâh	วีซ่า
visit *(places)* têe-o	เที่ยว
(people) yêe-um	เยี่ยม
voice sěe-ung	เสียง
voltage rairng fai fáh	แรงไฟฟ้า
wait ror	รอ
waiter kon sèrp	คนเสริฟ
waitress kon sèrp yǐng	คนเสริฟหญิง
Wales 'Wales'	เวลส์
wall *(inside)* fǎh	ฝา

   (outside) gum-pairng   กำแพง

wallet gra-bpǎo sa-dtahng   กระเป๋าสตางค์

warm òp ÒOn   อบอุ่น

washing powder pǒng súk fôrk   ผงซักฟอก

wasp dtairn   แตน

watch *(wrist-)* nah-li-gah kôr meu   นาฬิกาข้อมือ

water náhm   น้ำ

we rao   เรา

weather ah-gàht   อากาศ

wedding pi-tee dtàirng ngahn   พิธีแต่งงาน

week ah-tít   อาทิตย์

welcome: you're welcome mâi   ไม่เป็นไร
   bpen rai

west dta-wun dtòk   ตะวันตก

wet bpèe-uk   เปียก

what a-rai?   อะไร

wheel lór   ล้อ

when? mêu-a rai?   เมื่อไร

where? têe nǎi?   ที่ไหน

   where is ...? ... yòo têe nǎi?   ...อยู่ที่ไหน

which: which one? un nǎi?   อันไหน

whisky wít-sa-gêe   วิสกี้

white sěe kǎo   สีขาว

who? krai?   ใคร

why? tum-mai?   ทำไม

wide gwâhng   กว้าง

wife pun-ra-yah   ภรรยา

wind *(noun)* lom   ลม

window nâh-dtàhng   หน้าต่าง

with gùp   กับ

without mâi sài   ไม่ใส่

woman pôo-yǐng   ผู้หญิง

wood *(material)* mái   ไม้

wool kǒn sùt   ขนสัตว์

word kum   คำ

work *(noun)* ngahn   งาน

  (verb) tum ngahn   ทำงาน

  it's not working mun sěe-a   มันเสีย

write kěe-un   เขียน

  could you write it down?   ช่วยเขียนลงให้หน่อย

  chôo-ay kěe-un long hâi nòy, dâi   ได้ไหม

  mái?

wrong pìt   ผิด

year bpee   ปี

yellow sěe lěu-ung   สีเหลือง

yes *see page 7*

yesterday mêu-a wahn née   เมื่อวานนี้

yet: not yet yung   ยัง

you *(polite)* kOOn   คุณ

  (familiar) ter   เธอ

young *(man)*   หนุ่ม

  (woman)   สาว

  (child) dè   เด็กเล็ก

your(s) *(po...* kOOn   ...ของคุณ

  (familiar) ... kǒrng   ...ของเธอ

zip síp   ซิป